MOMENTS

OF CHOICE

My Path To Leadership

Moments of Choice: My Path To Leadership

Copyright © 2016 by Major General Linda Singh

ISBN: 978-0-9966531-2-1

Library of Congress Control Number: 2015919062

Writestream Publishing books may be ordered through booksellers.

Book design by Logotecture.

Printed in the United States of America.

Writestream Publishing, LLC
Parker Ford, PA
writestreampublishing.com

ACKNOWLEGEMENTS

First I would like to give glory to God Almighty for giving me the strength, perseverance, and faith to begin this journey.

I could not have shared the experiences, lessons, and knowledge contained in this book without the support of my family: My wonderful husband, Raj whom I will love forever, and my daughters Shaniece and Tara, who are my pride and joy. I am so very proud of both of you. I should also mention my dog children, TK who passed away, Thor, Scooby, and Xena who would often sit in my lap during my writing sessions, and our bird, Slash, who sings so beautifully just when I need it.

To my parents, thank you for bringing me into this world and allowing me to get to know such wonderful, loving, grandparents: Herbert and Genevieve Willis, to whom I probably owe the most. They took me in after raising 14 children of their own. I honor, love, and respect everything they did for me. May they rest in peace. I would also like to thank Ma and Pa Singh for giving birth to their wonderful son, who is now my soulmate.

To my extended family – the Willis', Dorms', Dorsey's, Costley's, Seeram's, Singh's, Carlton's, Smith's, Fresbie's and some other I am sure I have forgotten, I hope you know how much you mean to me. This includes my aunts and uncles who have at times also balanced between being my brothers, sisters, mother, and father. You have been such a vital part of my amazing life and were always there for me in whatever capacity I needed you.

To my coaches, teachers, and every Maryland community in which I have lived, thank you for your support during the times when, unknown to you, I really needed you. To my sisters, Sharon and Pam, thanks for the countless hours of honest conversation over the years. I probably don't say it enough, but I love you both.

To my civilian employer, Accenture, for whom I have worked over two decades, thank you for being there for me time and time again. I would also like to thank my coworkers with whom I have collaborated. Working with all of you has made it possible for me to grow endlessly. You have earned my respect in every way. It has been an amazing journey.

To my soldiers, airmen, civilian, and volunteer workforce in the Maryland Guard, you all ROCK. Don't you ever forget it.

While I would love to list all of my mentors by name, the list would simply be too long. Still, I want to thank each of you for believing in me, guiding me, giving me counsel, and most of all, allowing me to be me. Thank you.

And to the role models I have looked up to over the course of my life's journey, my deepest gratitude. Some of you may not even realize the impact you have made on me as an individual, but I will never forget. You have each inspired me in ways that words can't even describe.

To Daria and Lisa of Writestream Publishing, thank you for guiding me down this path. We have shared so much over the months and I hope you know how amazing you are.

For those of you who continue to support me, encourage me, and simply love me, thank you.

CONTENTS

MOMENTS OF CHOICE

My Path To Leadership

MAJOR GENERAL
LINDA SINGH

PROLOGUE

In January of 2012, I found myself standing in a trashy lot in Kabul, Afghanistan not far from our base, lost in the shocking despair and hopelessness of that environment. Although we were there to deliver clothing to the local villagers, it was one of those unforgettable times in my military service when I felt uncomfortable and even a little fearful. My senses – in what we often refer to as the "pucker factor" – were functioning at peak performance. The leads for Operation Outreach had told me I'd be surprised and touched by the experience when they asked me to assist this small support mission with one of the other teams. However to this day, I hadn't realized just how deeply it would affect me, notwithstanding the fact that I had grown up under economic conditions most Americans would describe as "underprivileged." Based on my own childhood and adolescence, I should have been prepared. But in my 48 years of life, I had never borne witness to such abject poverty.

The entire lot was lined with windowless, dilapidated buildings that were also missing doors – a great place to get ambushed. As I took it all in, I wondered if I had made the right decision. While every day outside the wire was somewhat tense, we were supposed to be in a fairly safe part of the country; this little excursion forced me to think twice about that security assessment. If this was considered "safe," I shuddered to think about what our troops in other parts of Afghanistan were facing. Unless you've been there yourself, you have no idea how your mind just takes over in these types of situations. Both mind and body go on high alert, sending danger signals and increasing your sense of awareness.

The first order I gave to my team that day was to remain vigilant and stay close together: under no circumstances should anyone wander off alone. I directed them, "Let's do what we came here to do and get the heck out of here." Since the dirt lot appeared to be vacant, I was also wondering if we came to the right place because it was supposed to be what the interpreter called a refugee camp.

We stood in a wide open space strewn with papers, bottles, and other assorted trash and surrounded by abandoned buildings, having entered through a designated area behind closed gates. Some of the structures featured makeshift walls of cardboard, plastic, and blankets – basically, anything the locals could find. Some windows were boarded up completely. For security reasons, we did not wander back in that area but remained out in the open.

In this desolate environment, there was no smell of "home," nor was there a single tree, flower, or plant growing anywhere. The place was definitely unnerving and as I stared at the large piles of concrete everywhere, I thought back to my grandparents' home in the Maryland countryside where I'd spent the first nine years of my life.

While the tiny house had just four rooms and lacked plumbing, we, at least, had a clean water source for bathing, drinking, and cooking. In stark contrast to this bleak Kabul community, we also had a yard with green grass and bursts of magnificent color provided by tulips, daffodils, and lilac and forsythia bushes. I remembered the many trees that also inhabited our yard and how green and alive they were in the summer before their leaves changed into vivid gold, red, and orange in the fall. By American standards, my childhood was marked by "poverty" but as I stood amid this Afghanistan scene wondering if these villagers even *had* a source of water, I fought back tears as I contemplated how blessed I was to be able to leave once I'd completed my assignment. I didn't have to *live* in this dreadful place.

We entered through a door connected to one of the walls. Once inside, it felt as if we were in a box with sides comprised of various buildings and barricades. I could see the local people peeking out from behind their makeshift enclosures just before male elders began to approach, escorting young children. As I watched, it became very clear to me that this was their life: simple yet stark. The familiar greetings they exchanged with our interpreter, one of our analysts who had grown up in Afghanistan, indicated that this was a place he would occasionally visit to drop off supplies. He introduced me and the rest of the group, which included two personnel from my team, one soldier and one contractor who pulled security, another soldier from our unit who worked with one of our generals, and two civilians who appeared to be somewhat overcome by the whole scene.

Our interpreter, of course, was familiar with all of the groups. He knew which local communities most needed our help – even if that help came only in the form of a small gesture of kindness. He facilitated the distribution process by organizing the clothing according to size and separating the children from the adults. Yet even this simple task was difficult. While he organized clothing, the other soldier and I had a short discussion about the environment, agreeing that we needed to finish our assignment as quickly as possible now that we were here. However, at the first sign of trouble, we would immediately vacate the area.

Our task became a little more challenging once we began handing out items mainly to the kids. It was interesting to observe their behavior as they selected articles of clothing that were noticeably too big for them. While we did experience a few problems keeping order and preventing them from rushing us in their excitement, our interpreter excelled at reestablishing discipline. In spite of everything, I couldn't help but feel a connection to these young Afghanistan children. I interacted with them mostly out of my belief that they will be the ones to make a difference in their country one day. When we saw their faces light up with joy and witnessed how much they wanted what we were offering – no matter how nonsensical – we couldn't help but smile. We didn't care what they were going to do with these gifts: all that mattered was that we were there to provide them.

It reminded me again of how fortunate I'd been at their age, even though we were not well off. There's poverty and then there's *poverty*: what I saw unfolding before me bore no resemblance to my life in the United States at any point, not even as a young girl in rural Maryland living in a four-room house with no plumbing. True, the life I'm currently living is a far cry from my humble beginnings. Yet even my early years seemed privileged when compared to the bleak circumstances these children lived under every day in Kabul.

In spite of the horrors taking place everywhere else in Afghanistan, this was one of those days I'll always remember for its sheer impact. It helped to ground me in humility, compassion, and appreciation for everything I had.

We all live our lives in various ways. We experience many different situations that may lead us to think we have failed. But we must remember that these outcomes are a direct result of the choices we make and those that are sometimes made *for* us. Regardless of how these choices occur, they determine what the next branch in our life's tree will look like. These branches form the various pathways we'll embark upon throughout our time on Earth. Whenever a particular branch leads us to a dead end, we often become so preoccupied with the fact that the path has ended that we don't even bother to look around for other paths or branches.

Yet if we open our minds and eyes, sometimes what may

seem like a dead end can lead to another multitude of choices. Ultimately, it all comes down to making the best choice possible with the information we have at any given point in time. For the individuals living in that Kabul village, their choices are simple and profound: to live the best way they know how, to survive another day, and to obtain enough food to feed their families. For most of us in the free world, however, such basic considerations are a given. In Afghanistan, a villager's choice can be yanked away at any second by virtue of being a product of their environment, or a casualty of a conflict.

As Americans, we tend to take our freedom of choice for granted and/or waste it on senseless things. Because actions have consequences, we pay for these choices in a myriad of ways but, for the most part, our decisions can lead us to productive, meaningful lives. Residents of Afghanistan don't have this luxury; their choices are severely limited and in no way compare to those enjoyed by American citizens. My brief but insightful view of a day in the life of an Afghanistan village was all I needed to know that I am truly blessed.

CHAPTER 1

THE EARLY YEARS - LITTLE HOUSE IN THE COUNTRY

As a young child, I did not understand or even think about poverty. This was in spite of the fact that I spent the first nine years of my life in the four-room house where my grandmother was born; the place where she raised her own children. During my childhood, there were times when ten or more of us lived together under my grandparents' roof, yet not once did I ever consider myself poor.

I am sure that being the youngest clouded my perspective of things but if there were challenges with all of the mouths to feed, my grandparents – whom I lovingly called "Mom-mom" and "Pop-pop" – kept it to themselves. I never remember them complaining about keeping the grandkids or feeding other family members who would come to visit on the weekends. From what I can recall, it was the place where everyone loved to meet up; weekends all throughout the year were filled with plenty of family. Our home was situated in the countryside of Frederick County Maryland, near Buffalo Road. The tiny home I came to know and love dearly rested amid beautiful woods, flower beds, grass, and fields. Because it was full of love, I never wanted for anything.

Downstairs there was a kitchen/eating area and another room

with a divider wall that separated a family room in the front and on the other side, my grandparents' bedroom.

Upstairs were two sleeping areas and if I remember correctly, about eight beds. There also was an attic where I'd been told a boogey man resided. The best part of the house? The tin roof, especially when it rained.

While the house did not have running water, there was a spring just down the hill on the 26 acres that comprised my grandparents' property. With no indoor plumbing, we had the minimum daily task (which often became necessary multiple times a day depending upon usage) of going down the hill to retrieve water for cooking, cleaning, and bathing. I hated this job only because there used to be a huge spider that would nest on the rocks during spring, summer, and fall. I swear it was so enormous I could see its beady eyes. Even though I knew it was a different spider each year it didn't matter: it was still scary.

As you might imagine, with no indoor plumbing even the simplest things required more effort. When you have running water, you can very easily jump in the shower and run bath water. But in our case, planning was necessary to ensure enough hot water for everyone. An activity as simple as taking a bath brought on a whole new meaning: in order to bathe in our home, you had to learn how to effectively take a bird bath or in other words, bathe in a metal tub. Since I was young, my grandmother or my aunt took on the laborious, time-consuming process of preparing my bath by heating large amounts of water on the stove.

On Sundays, I had the privilege of using the big tub to take a bath. I would climb in, get wet, and then wash and rinse several times. After I was done and dried off, my grandmother and aunt would use another reserve of water to wash my hair. I hated this part of the weekly ritual because I had a *ton* of hair. I would have to lay across two chairs, letting my head hang into the tub so they could shampoo it. While washing a thick head of hair was difficult, it was actually the easiest part; combing it out took forever. My patient grandmother would painstakingly comb it out section by section, using Royal Crown to grease it. Oh did I say grease my *hair*, I meant grease my *head*. She would use so much of the stuff you could squeeze some out for use the next day! But let me tell you, I had beautiful hair during that time. My favorite style, one I wore often, was one plait in the front and two in the back.

Did I mention that the lack of indoor plumbing also meant there were just two options when nature called? Either use a pot or go to the outhouse. I definitely hated using the outhouse in the middle of the night and in the summer. If you needed to go to the bathroom in the middle of the night or whenever it was dark, you had to take the flashlight and walk to the outhouse – which was, at least, a couple of hundred yards away from the house. It wouldn't have mattered to me if the outhouse had been right next door; when you are a little kid, everything seems far away when you are alone in the dark. Typically, I'd wake up my aunt or get someone to go with me. Sometimes after I'd entered the outhouse, they'd pretend they were going to leave just to get a rise out of me. In the summertime, my dislike of the outhouse stemmed from the fact that there always seemed to be a menacing spider inside, right above the door.

By now you have probably have figured out that I don't like spiders at all. My arachnophobia's source is an incident that occurred when I was playing school and creating a pretend science project. As a little kid, I was always trying to be like my uncles and would attempt to do the same things they did. One day I was collecting insects – butterflies, beetles, worms – you name it and trying to pin them to a piece of cardboard. That's when I got the "bright" idea to catch a spider, which turned out to be not so bright because I got bit and ended up with a huge spot on my leg that required lancing. That was no fun at all, especially because I don't think I knew that spiders would bite. From that point on I developed a fear of them but still loved to play with granddaddy long legs, the one spider species that fascinated me. Other favorite creatures included frogs, crayfish, and turtles.

Once I was playing in the house with a frog, I'd caught in the creek and it got away. My grandmother was like, "Hon, didn't I tell you not to bring that frog in the house; you better catch it and put it outside!" By that time, it had jumped under a chair in the corner of the kitchen. As I reached my hand under the chair, retrieved the frog, and pulled it back out again, there was the biggest spider I'd ever seen in my life just sitting there on my hand. Immediately I dropped the frog and started shaking my hand and jumping around like a crazy person. My heart was beating so fast I am lucky I didn't have a heart attack. Needless to say, this little incident did nothing to alleviate my fear of spiders and in fact, probably made it worse.

But spiders weren't my only reason for being afraid of the dark. Some of my uncles were practical jokers who got a kick out of scaring me. They would make noises and tell me that the boogey man – who lived in our attic – was going to get me if I wasn't a good girl. As a result, I would sometimes dare my brother and sister to go up in the attic with me when they would come to visit. We would make it to the first step or two, then jump down and run for our lives. If we made it all the way to the top to push up the board to look in, we considered the effort to be a success. One time I went the distance, pushed the wood from over the steps, and looked up in the attic before I heard something, jumped down, and bolted. More than anything I think I scared myself. Unfortunately, in my rush to escape I forgot to put the wood back – not a good thing because while the boogey man was probably not living in our attic, several bats were residing there. You can imagine my delight later on when I came upstairs to go to bed, only to discover a bat flying around!

If you think *that* was something, one summer morning I was coming down the stairs (which, by the way, did not have any lights) and nearly stepped on a snake that was coiled up on the very last step. Naturally, I was quick to rush back up to the second floor screaming for someone to get the broom to take care of the problem, else I would try to jump over the snake to get the broom and remove it myself.

There were also times when our attic's bat population would cause a lot of excitement by escaping their confines and flying around upstairs. Trying to get these creatures out was quite an ordeal. If you happened to be in bed, you'd simply throw the covers over your head with hopes that someone else would succeed in removing them from the premises.

Notwithstanding the occasional bat and snake problems, when it wasn't cold outside mornings were my favorite part the day. During the frigid months of the year, I hated to leave the warmth of my covers but once I did, I'd run to the foot of the bed to stand by the stove pipe and warm up. In the early hours of winter mornings, I'd always hear someone – either one of my grandparents or my aunt – stoking the wood in the stove in the kitchen area, which was used to cook meals and heat the house. Featuring a steel top with a multitude of burners, an oven, and several doors the old, large white stove took up most of the kitchen. Although this huge appliance was way too big for such a small space, it was functional and served a variety of purposes, with one end used for dish water and the other for meal preparation.

However, in the summertime, it was not optimal because in order to cook there had to be a fire burning in the stove. That meant that unless you wanted to be extremely hot and sweaty, you'd choose to spend more time either outside or upstairs. While I'm not sure exactly how high the temperature would climb in the kitchen during the humid months of summer, I do remember it was stifling and uncomfortable. Ever the champs, my grandmother and aunt would cook inside even on the most sweltering days. To minimize the heat, they would try to prepare and cook our food early in the day.

Once in a while, the stove would get so hot and the fire so high that the chimney would catch fire. I remember going upstairs occasionally to feel the chimney to determine if it was overheating. One particular day when it caught fire, it necessitated a visit from the fire department – a scary occurrence because if anything had happened to our house, I am not sure what we would have done. Perhaps that's why my grandfather or one of the boys would often storm into the kitchen scolding my grandmother and aunt for letting the fire get too hot while cooking.

Needless to say, we did not have air-conditioning – not even window units. Even if we'd had them, I doubt our fuse box could have supported them. Yes, I did say *fuse box* and *not* a breaker box. We got by with window fans for the upstairs and downstairs windows. These fans fascinated me; I would get close to them to sing into them because I liked the way it would make my voice sound. But I didn't stop there. Sometimes I would put playing cards in the fan just to hear the clicking sound it would make when I held one end of a card in my hand and let other end interact with the spinning blades. Now that I think about it, it was not very safe. Whenever my grandfather caught me in the act, he would scold me, but it never seemed to stop me completely.

By far, my favorite meals were on the weekends when my aunt, whom I called "Sissie," would fry chicken and make potato salad and greens. While I can't be certain if she cooked with lard, I know that even to this day old-fashioned fried chicken cooked on a wood stove is simply the best. My aunt would spend the entire morning frying chicken – probably three or four whole ones in all – and we would end up with a copious amount of it, along with maybe ten pounds' worth of potato salad to feed the numerous people who were constantly in and out of our house. Another of my favorite meals, prepared by my grandmother, was liver and onions; for some odd reason I loved the taste, even as a little kid. It was especially good when it was cooked dry and cold – my favorite leftovers. Although I don't eat it as often now, I still enjoy liver.

No matter how dire our financial situation, we always had more than enough food to eat: my grandparents always saw to that. They never turned anyone away and would always offer them a home-cooked meal.

Calls of Nature Answered in the Outhouse

Since we did not have indoor plumbing, we kept a pot indoors. For those who are wondering, it truly is a pot one uses in place of a toilet. However, unlike a toilet the pot is only designed for one function; therefore, in our house if you had to do number two you had to go to the outhouse. That was the worst for me because I was afraid of the dark. I made an effort to do my business before going to sleep but for whatever reason, I had problems waking up in the middle of the night and would regularly wet the bed at least once per week. With the benefit of hindsight, I now believe there was a deeply rooted issue in my subconscious causing this childhood problem, but no matter when it happened my family never made me feel bad.

Despite my embarrassment, I didn't know how to make it stop even though it didn't happen every night. The fact that I was afraid of the dark may have played a part in the bedwetting issue because even when getting up to use the pot I wanted to turn the light on. With four other people sleeping in the room this was problematic; inevitably, turning on the light would wake at least one of them. Outhouse trips in the middle of the night required an adult escort – usually Sissie – but if it was early evening, I went by myself. I hated the outhouse for the many reasons already discussed but also because it smelled in the summer.

Fortunately for me, my uncles were tasked with keeping it clean. Although I would watch them shovel the waste into buckets, I have no idea where they disposed of it. Even though I'd bear witness to this unpleasant but necessary springtime ritual, I definitely didn't like to help. Regardless of how distasteful, it was just one of the many required chores around our house.

Love, Laundry, and Lightning Rods

Doing laundry was another major event in our house, managed by my grandmother and aunt. First, the clothes had to be sorted to determine how many loads would be needed. Then the boys would have to fetch water from the spring, resulting in at least five or more containers of water sitting in the yard. Most of the buckets held five gallons, but there was also a smaller one just for me because I liked to help. In the beginning, I'd have to stop part of the way up the hill but eventually, I developed the strength to carry my half-full bucket to the top. Sometimes when one of my uncles was hauling a five-gallon bucket filled to capacity, I would get on the other side and hold the handle to "assist" him – even though all of the boys were strong enough to carry them on their own. My grandmother would use the metal buckets to heat the water needed; she'd repeat this process until she washed all of the clothes.

The chore of doing laundry was made even more difficult due to the fact that the wash machine was located in our tiny kitchen – along with the stove, wood pile, refrigerator, table, and a small couch. This didn't leave much room for many people to begin with but when washing clothes, the wash machine – a tub washer with ringers at the top, had to be pulled away from the wall. My grandmother and aunt put the clothes into the washer, then plugged it in to start the wash. When the load was finished, they would begin feeding the clothes through the rollers, which we called ringers. The clothes would then be rinsed and sent through the ringer again. That was my favorite part of doing laundry: ringing the clothes. Occasionally, it was my assigned job. I liked to help feed the clothes through the ringer but understood how important it was to keep your hands clear of the rollers themselves.

Once the laundry was done, we'd take it out to the yard where about four or five rows of clotheslines (I can't recall exactly how many) awaited us, along with a large bucket of clothespins we would use to fasten them. Although this was fun for me (I loved to hide in between the clothes or control the clothespin bucket so I could hand out the pins), I have no doubt it was a laborious amount of work for my grandmother. It was also my job to check on the clothes as they hung outside on the lines to determine if they were dry. How I loved to breathe in their fresh, clean scent! It left such a sensory impression in my memory that I kept this tradition into my early adult years until I moved into an apartment where it was no longer possible to hang laundry outside.

Still, even the enjoyable task of laundry was fraught with a certain amount of peril. In the summer, taking the clothes off the line could result in getting stung by the bees that loved to hide in them; in the frigid cold of winter, the clothes would dry stiff and hard. Sometimes we'd have clothes hanging from all lines when a storm approached and threatened to drench them in the rain, forcing several of us (typically led my aunt or one of the boys) to run out and rescue them before the deluge.

Summertime storms in Maryland could be pretty intense. When it would just rain, you could stand under the large walnut tree in the yard and if the leaves were full, not get wet at all; we would just hang out on the porch until it stopped. But whenever we had a violent storm the power would go out; if it happened when it was dark outside we'd light the kerosene lamp. My grandfather held firmly to the belief that when lightning and thunder made an appearance, you needed to sit down and remain quiet out of respect for the Almighty. During thunderstorms, we'd play cards by the kerosene lamp while talking softly. My favorite card game was *Solitaire* or *Go Fish*.

During the quiet periods of the storms, you could hear the pitter-patter of rain falling on the tin roof – a most heavenly sound. Nothing else you can imagine is quite so peaceful. Even if the power stayed on, my grandfather would still direct us to turn everything off out of fear of lightning inflicting irreparable damage. I used to think he was joking until one year an especially harsh storm with severe lightning caused a chimney fire, thanks to the lightning rods on our house (its only source of grounding). Luckily the fire did not amount to anything significant. While the experience of lightning hitting the house was terrifying for me as a kid, it did teach me to have a healthy respect for thunderstorms.

In addition to lightning rods, we also had an antenna with a wire leading to the TV, which could also attract lightning. This antenna was yet another crazy feature of the home that created an interesting task for me: going out to turn it in an effort to clear the TV picture when needed. I would stay out there as they hollered directives through the window as to when to stop turning. Our TV was black and white; I am not even certain when I first had the opportunity to watch a color TV. It was not the best, nor was it large. It also lacked knobs, forcing us to use pliers to turn the channel. Still, it was good enough to watch my favorite shows: *Bonanza*, *The Flintstones*, *The Wonderful World of Disney*, *The Wild, Wild West*, *Petty Coat Junction*, and *Scooby Doo*. My grandparents' favorites? *The Ed Sullivan Show* and *The Carol Burnett Show*.

Food, Fun and Fond Memories

Some of my most treasured memories are intertwined with the various seasons and times of the year. If you didn't grow up in the country – or at the very least with gardens and animals, it's hard to appreciate or understand this statement. In the spring, the flowers in the yard would bloom all over, thanks in part to my grandmother's green thumb. There were tulips, daffodils, bluebells, forsythia and lilac bushes, fruit trees, pussy willows, snowball bushes, and roses among many others. It was the time of the year that we would begin the planting season, which meant after my grandfather came home from work or from picking up my grandmother, he would labor in the garden.

I used to think rocks had the ability to grow on their own because every year we'd spend a significant amount of time picking them up in order to plant. My grandfather would run the tractor with the hair rake and then plow rows for planting. I enjoyed dropping the seeds for peas, corn, string beans and squash, and planting potatoes and bulbs for onions, beets, etc. While I know my contribution did not comprise the hardest part of the process, I did my best to help wherever allowed. I loved to watch the garden grow and checked on it all the time, impatiently waiting for things to begin sprouting. Once the corn grew high, you'd often find me hiding among the stalks eating raw corn, spring onions, or turnips. But my most favorite of all were the juicy garden tomatoes; something I adore to this day.

Aside from the blooming flowers and copious vegetable garden, spring also signified the arrival of Easter, one of my favorite holidays. Easter was wonderful because I would get a new dress which my grandmother either made by hand or bought especially for me. It was also the time of the year when if I needed a new bike, I would get one, but my favorite gifts were the Easter bunnies – pink, white, and chocolate, that were given to me by my Aunt Emily and Uncle Petie. While it may seem to be a small, insignificant gesture, I have fond memories of visiting them one Easter and receiving those treasured bunnies.

During the summer, I liked being outside all day long climbing trees, playing games and taunting insects and bees. Even in the country, there are things you can get into that may be ill-advised. I would catch beetles or bumble bees, tie a string on their leg, and let them fly. Sometimes I would have three or four. I also liked to catch fireflies in a jar to bring them in the house at night to watch them light up.

My favorite outdoor game was *Cowboys and Indians* but more frequently than not you'd find me just sitting up in the maple tree out in the yard – my favorite place to be as high up as I could possibly go. Yes, I was definitely a tomboy. I remember getting mad one summer because I could not walk around with my shirt off like my uncles who worked in the yard and showed off their muscles. Since I wanted to be like them, I took off my shirt, only to have my grandmother scold me.

Summertime was great because I could do something many of today's kids sadly don't – play in the yard all day. Back then there were no computers so engaging in outdoor activities was my only option. I was good at playing by myself because I discovered an endless array of fun things to do in the woods like playing house, making mud pies, or hunting for bugs. Sometimes on the weekends, my grandfather would have to go to Unionville to get gas for the tractor or lawn mower, or to take in the soda pop bottles in exchange for more sodas. Unionville was about 15 minutes from where we lived and both were off of Route 26. During that time if you returned the bottle, you received money back – I think it was five cents or something like that.

Invariably he would get gas at the same general store in the town. I always wanted to go with him because that was where I could get candy cigarettes, fireballs, wax candy, and bubble gum. I would purchase twenty-five cents' worth of candy, which was generous amount – at least in my estimation. As I walked out of the store with a little brown bag of candy just for me, I felt very proud. Aside from candy, I would also get to have a Coke in the small bottles and drink it before I even left the store. One year, 1971 I believe, the Coca-Cola plant hosted a contest. There were plastic circles under the bottle caps you needed to collect in order to get a copy of the 45 record featuring the song, *I'd Like to Teach the World to Sing*. Since I was hell-bent on collecting 100 of those plastic tops, I had everyone saving them for me. My grandfather took me to the Coca-Cola plant in Frederick where I got my very first record – which was that song – and I have loved drinking Coke ever since.

Funny, I did not remember this sweet event in my young life until about 2010 when I was in a women's international fellowship program. We were doing a reflection type of exercise and two of us were talking about our love for Coke when simultaneously we both began singing, *I'd Like to Teach the World to Sing*. For reasons obvious to me now, I started to cry; at that moment, it hit me why I have such a fondness for Coca-Cola. The realization brought forth a reservoir of deep, palpable emotions.

Growing up, as summer neared its end we'd begin our preparations for winter. This meant we would cut a tremendous amount of wood while my grandmother would can vegetables, dig up the bulbs before the big freeze for certain flowers, put plastic on the windows in preparation for the cold, and set up the oil-burning stove in one of the rooms. These were the tasks I remember most. One year, my grandfather was cutting down trees in an area we referred to as "The Bottom" – the bottom of a hill further in the woods past a bunch of old, decaying cars which made it rather scary for me, at least, when I was little.

As he worked, the chainsaw he'd been using hit a knot and bounced back into his knee. Thankfully, although the cut went all the way to the bone, it did not cut *into* the bone. The boys carried him up to the house to take him to the doctor. Even though I was petrified, I thanked God he was alright and that his injury wasn't worse. My grandmother, as always, handled it like a champ and went into action just like she did with everything. She was a remarkably strong lady who was constantly doing; I'm pretty sure I got some of my energy from her. It seemed she knew how to do everything even though she was not highly educated. Both she and my grandfather knew how to provide for their family...and they did it well.

During canning season, Mom-mom would prep all of the vegetables and fruits, can them, and put them in the cellar for the winter. Wooden shelves in the cellar displayed the canned food she'd prepared along with store-bought items. There would also be huge piles of potatoes that seemed to last for a good period. The tiny, shallow cellar was comprised of dirt and located under the house, with one string light illuminating the area. Which brings me back to the lights inside the house. Unlike the lights in many homes today, ours were not operated by a switch. Each light had to be turned on individually by a push switch, turn switch, pull chain, or simply by plugging them in, which was the case for the porch lights.

We also had several apple trees, pear trees, and plum trees. While the apples were used for all kinds of mouth-watering creations, my most favorite (as I think it was for everyone) were the apple dumplings my grandmother made. Featuring plenty of dough around the perimeter – their best feature – these dumplings tasted indescribably delicious. In all of my years of life, I've yet to meet anyone who can make apple dumplings like my grandmother. Every week or so she also baked cakes from scratch, along with applesauce and apple butter. I would help her by picking the apples; she would cut them up and cook them. Then she'd use a food mill to churn them, converting them into sauce and depending on the ingredients, apple butter.

However, her most famous culinary creation was called a "wacky cake," derived from a recipe passed down through the generations. While Mom-mom did not even have the written recipe, she'd obviously committed it well to memory because boy was it ever scrumptious! You have not eaten chocolate cake until you've tasted my grandmother's wacky cake. Sometimes she'd frost it with white icing but I preferred it plain and cold. There is only one person in our family today, Aunt Emily, who knows how to make that cake the way my grandmother did.

The late fall was also a time when my grandfather would go hunting for rabbit, squirrel, coon, pheasant, and even groundhog. If you have never had them, it is something you really should try. Rabbit and squirrel are best prepared fried and smothered in gravy. These are delicacies you should simply eat and not think much about. I would help my grandfather skin and clean them. He would slit the skin around the middle and then pull towards the head and tail. I would get to pull on one side and he would then chop off the feet and head. Then you'd slit them down the belly to clean the insides. While many may regard this practice as cruel, when it comes down to whether or not you have a meal to eat, you quickly get over it. It was this type of game that helped to stretch things from one day to the next.

Whenever they would go after coon, it had to be dark. Once, I remember Uncle Bubby went out and shot a coon, but it scurried back up the tree. He came back to get a flashlight because he thought it might have fallen on the ground. However, it turned out the coon was way up a hole in the tree. My uncle waited until the next morning to see if he could get it with a ladder. No luck; it was still too high. Undaunted, he then recruited me to climb up and over his back and stand on his shoulders to see if I could grab the tail, with the instructions to fling it just in case it was only hurt. Needless to say, that coon provided another family meal.

Some Thanksgivings we'd eat pheasant or quail but most of the time fresh turkey from a farm. During this time, Pop-pop would also help one of his good friends, Mr. Mack, slaughter hogs. They would forbid me to watch when they'd take them down but did allow me to observe while they cleaned them. I guess you can tell by now that I was definitely not a queasy kid; on the contrary, I was an adventurous one. The Mack's also had a hen house where Ms. Margret would tend to the chickens. I would sometimes help her by going to the hen house to collect the eggs or feed the chickens.

Occasionally the chickens were highly uncooperative; in fact, they could be downright hostile and often chased me out of the hen house. There was one rooster that was so mean he would attack you anytime you got near the place. It seemed he would stand watch over the entire area and sense precisely when I was approaching in spite of my best efforts to be stealthy. I'd try to sneak up to the door and get in before he'd notice. It became a game – one I'd lose when I'd get stuck in the hen house peeking out until I saw him walk away.

The Mack's always had plenty of animals on their little farm. One year Mr. Mack rescued a flying squirrel. From that point on, it would crawl up in his pants leg to hide and he would have to grab it before it got too far. One of my fondest memories of spending time at the Mack's is getting to hold and play with that squirrel.

From an early age, I developed a love and appreciation for animals, probably because we had so many of our own. Based on a story my grandmother once told me, it seemed that on one particular occasion I was chasing a "cat" until I finally got close enough to coax it to me. What my child's mind failed to comprehend was that this was not a cat at all. Apparently, I had chased a skunk instead, one that for some inexplicable reason allowed me to get way too close. The feeling was definitely mutual so you can imagine what happened. Ah, the life of a country girl.

CHAPTER 2

FAMILY INFLUENCES – THE JOY OF BELONGING

I lived with my grandparents from the time I was three months old until my ninth birthday. Because I was with them all the time, I was an old soul at heart. Honestly, I don't know how they dealt so well with the lack of privacy that typified daily life in our home. Since the enormous wood stove took up most of the room in the kitchen, the remaining space on the first floor was partitioned into two rooms: a sitting area and another area I hesitate to even describe as my grandparents' bedroom. It barely accommodated their bed and two dressers, along with a pot they would bring into the room only at night. Being a prying little thing, I'd often sneak in and jump into bed with them. Sometimes when I fell asleep in there, one of my uncles or Sissie would have to come get me and take me upstairs. In our house, we lived by the adage, "early to bed, early to rise." Most of us were asleep by 8 p.m. and up by 5 a.m. but I was allowed to "sleep in" until 6 a.m.

Mom-mom was a small woman who had given birth to 17 children, 14 of whom survived. She'd been born in the house in which she'd also raised her kids – the same one I lived in during the early part of my childhood. While I only have vague memories of her mother, my great-grandmother, I do recall she was elderly.

For the longest time, I thought she was white. In reality, she was mixed-race.

A hard-working woman, Mom-mom kept house for several families and judging from what I observed, they treated her well. Oftentimes, she'd arrive home bearing gifts from her customers – bags of clothes, toys, and other items. One family, in particular, would send me Matzo's and a variety of other treats throughout the year though Matzo's were my favorites. When I think about it now, my early love of Matzo's was a precursor to my enjoyment of the crackers in the military, probably because of their similarities.

Although Mom-mom split her work time between various customers, she never complained and seldom missed a day as far as I can recall. Yet when she'd arrive home, she'd immediately head to the kitchen to cook dinner if Sissie hadn't already started meal preparation.

My grandfather, a tall, slender man, had brown skin with red undertones. He'd served in the Navy during World War II and worked for Fort Detrick, where he took care of the animals used for research. I remember him telling stories about how they would sometimes bite him. Eventually, Pop-pop retired from Fort Detrick, freeing him to drive Mom-mom to work in the mornings and pick her up in the evenings.

On Tuesdays and Thursdays, my Aunt Shirley (who was also my godmother) rode with them because her husband, my Uncle Rob, had to get to work early. So he'd drop her off at our house and much to my delight I'd get to see them during the week *and* on the weekends in most cases. My godparents were incredibly special to me; I loved spending time with them. On several occasions Aunt Shirley would present me with little gifts – ribbons for my hair, chewing gum, Avon samples, clothes, and other items. When she chewed gum, she would somehow make it snap, inspiring me to work hard at this skill in an effort to emulate her. I was so proud once I learned how to do it because I thought it made me just like her.

Uncle Rob, my godfather, always had a cigar in his mouth though it was rarely ever lit. For this reason, I am not even sure how much he ever smoked them. However, one time I went to jump on him when the cigar actually was lit, causing me to burn my arm. Even now I still have a light mark there from the incident which I don't mind at all because it reminds me of him.

Company aside, visiting my godparents was fun because they lived near train tracks. From inside their house, you could hear the train as it approached, prompting me to run down the hill to get a close-up view whenever I was there. One time, Uncle Rob and Aunt Shirley even took me for a ride on the train because they knew it fascinated me. During a recent trip to the train museum in downtown Baltimore, looking at the multitude of train displays brought back many fond memories I had long forgotten about.

My godparents lived next door to my Aunt Hazel and Uncle Kenny. Since Rob and Kenny were brothers, sometimes, I'd visit with them too. Back then it seemed customary to take care of your parents because several of these couples had one parent living with them. In this case, the mothers-in-law lived with their daughters and they too were like surrogate grandmothers to me. As far as I was concerned they were family; I couldn't have possibly loved them more if they'd been blood relatives. Funny, because I was the baby I spent more time with my grandparents their own children did during those years. In fact, my first nine years of life were heavily influenced by my uncles and aunts. As the youngest female, living in a mostly male household unmistakably shaped my comfort level in normal, everyday life; it formed the foundation not only for the games we'd all play and how we played them but also the acceptable degree of roughness.

For me, the best time of the year was always late spring,

summer, and early fall. That's when we spent a significant amount of time outdoors and escaped the confines of our tiny house which felt terribly cramped in the winter. Being both a girl and the youngest in the family meant I often got my way – with some exceptions, of course. If I wanted to be around the boys, then I had to *be* like the boys. This included full participation in "boyish" activities like boxing. One of my most vivid memories centers around the time one of my uncles got a pair of boxing gloves and they would all box and joke around. I desperately wanted to learn how to box – so learn I did. Ever accommodating, my uncles would put the gloves on me and we'd go at it. Or more specifically they'd hit me, then I would get mad and throw punches. The problem was, I'd forget all about the form they'd previously taught me just to get in a hit. Whenever they'd put their hands on my head to hold me back, I'd simply resist and keep fighting, needlessly burning energy. Finally, they'd settle me down well enough to teach me how to hold my hands, block a punch, throw a cross punch, jab, and uppercut. They even taught me the proper footwork. And while I never did become a boxer, the experience empowered me to defend myself; from that point on, I was never afraid to stand up to a bully.

Although I thoroughly enjoyed my boxing lessons, I never thought they would come in handy. However, a number of years later when I was around 12 or 13 years old and living under my parents' roof my mother was admitted to the hospital for appendicitis, forcing my sister Pam and me to stay with our Great Aunt Jessie (our mother's aunt) in a rough section of Washington. Little did we know, this would be our first *and* last big trip to the city for the foreseeable future. Inexplicably, Aunt Jessie made us wear dresses that day in spite of the fact that Pam and I both hated them. So there we were out in the park playing – my sister, my brother, and me when two or three teenage boys approached us. Since we could tell they were trouble just by looking at them, we immediately tried to get away. We raced into a building and ran as fast as we possibly could before we took a wrong turn and ran into a dead end; at that point it was just my sister and me, cornered. At that moment, the only thing I remember was palpable fear and powerful adrenaline pulsating through my body, spurring me into action. I came out fighting and threw punches as hard as I could so we could all get past them and make it back to the security of our aunt's apartment. Well, I can safely say my *fight or flight* response took them by surprise and forced them to back off just enough to make our escape but let me tell you: I am positive I would have fought to the bitter end if it had been necessary.

As I mentioned, growing up with seven- to- eight boys in the house at any given time is bound to have some level of influence on a young girl. Aside from boxing, they played basketball, soccer, football, baseball or softball, ping pong, and badminton. Consequently, I learned to play all of these sports at an early age in my never-ending effort to be one of them. My favorite sport by far, however, was basketball. I would practice around the clock to improve my form and develop my skills so they would let me play with them, but there was always one problem: I was simply too small to play with the big guys when a serious game was at stake. Our basketball court was comprised of dirt with a plywood backboard and rim that sometimes featured a net but most of the time did not. The boys would play almost every day, but all I could do was sit and watch until they finished the game. My passion for sports remained with me as I entered high school, where I continued to play.

My involvement in my high school basketball team had its roots in elementary school. When I was in the sixth grade, one of my gym teachers also coached the junior varsity team at Linganore High School, which serves the eastern portion of Frederick County. She advised me to try out for the team once I reached the ninth grade, the year of eligibility. Sure enough, a few years later I made

Linganore High's basketball team in my freshman year. Although I also ran track and cross country, basketball was my first love.

The day I made the team is one I'll never forget. Because I didn't own any high tops, I wore an old pair of Uncle Bernard's converse sneakers which of course were way too big. To make them fit better, I put on multiple pairs of socks and tied up the laces as tightly as I could. Once on the J.V. team, I enjoyed the unwavering support of my wonderful coaches, one of whom – the junior varsity coach – would regularly pick me up and drive me home from practice, even though it was well out of his way.

My parents and my uncle Bernard attended my very first game. In honor of the occasion, Uncle Bernard presented me with a brand new pair of white leather converse high tops before the contest got underway. Thrilled with my new shoes that actually fit properly, I showed off my skills throughout the entire game but fouled out in the last quarter. As I recall, I finished with about 12 rebounds and 10 points – a respectable result for junior varsity in those days. Boy, do I remember that year well. I felt such incredible pride and absolute certainty that I would end up starting the next year because I was a good player who could hold her own on the court. By the end of my first year on J.V., they promoted me to varsity because our varsity team was headed to the championship. I continued to play basketball until I left Linganore in my eleventh-grade year. Even though I did not get to finish out playing at my high school, I am still a Lancer through and through.

Because I was such a tomboy, I always climbed trees, ran in the woods, swung on vines, played cops and robbers, and enjoyed playing with toy guns. No doubt, my favorite television shows like *The Wild Wild West* featuring the characters James West and Artemis Gordon (played by Robert Conrad and Ross Martin, respectively) influenced my preferences. I could watch replays of this show all day long but then couldn't wait to get outside and reenact the whole episode. It was one of my favorite role-play games and whenever my brother and sister would visit, I'd get them to play along with me. However, I would always have to be James because, in my mind, he was the absolute best. Even back then I liked to be the good guy and never the bad guy. For a significant time period, this was an obsession for me in that I wanted six-shooters, a belt, and a cowboy hat and boots.

Pop-pop eventually bought me a pair of toy six-shooters – cap guns I would wear while outside playing. Caps were the best because you didn't have to run around yelling "Bang, bang!" They would actually fire. I'd pretend my bike was a horse and ride around pretending to catch bad guys. Even when my brother and sister weren't around, I'd entertain myself for hours with this game, using dolls and teddy bears to play the different parts. But as I'd learn one day, even the most proficient, gun-toting good guy can get into a jam requiring the assistance of another good guy.

I must've been little because my great-grandmother was still alive at the time. After I had donned one of my uncle's long raincoats along with my six shooters, hat, and bandanna, I recruited her to play with me and asked her to pretend I was coming to rescue her from the bad guy (the dog) in my role as James West. Proudly, I strode out to our road and down to the end of the woods where I climbed several trees and began to jump from one to the other (in my mind, going from building to building) as I prepared to make my grand entrance and "save" my great grandmother. However, there was one big problem: the dog. Once I pulled out my guns and began to shoot he went crazy, pulling at my coat, growling, and trying to throw me to the ground. My poor old great grandmother did her best to get the dog off as I started pulling off the coat, glasses, and gun to show him it was me. Nevertheless, he kept chasing me to the point where I had to climb up the maple tree to get away from him.

Finding My Purpose

After my Sunday bath ritual, I loved to watch *The Wonderful World of Disney* in the early evening with my family. We'd all sit around and watch, and once the show was over it was my bedtime. As I mentioned, we all retired pretty early in those days. The only thing that extended my bedtime once in a while was a visit from my aunts and uncles in Westminster; I was allowed to stay up until they left. I loved seeing them because it meant I could hang out with my cousins who were all around the same age. Even though my aunts and uncles all had their own children, they always made me feel incredibly special; I was their "Little Lindy," their "Boo," or their "Annie Oakley" depending on each one's preference. To my grandparents, I was "Bugs."

Uncle Joe and Aunt Joan lived on Old Chapel Road outside of Westminster and would pick me up on some weekends. One time very close to Christmas they took me to see the amazing Barnum and Bailey Circus. They also gave me a Barbie doll (yes, I played with dolls too), though my favorite was paper dolls. I had tons of them. To Uncle Joe I was his "Little Lindy" and even though he is no longer with us today, Auntie Joan still refers to me that way on occasion.

While to this point I have not discussed my parents in much detail, they were involved in my life. Whenever they came to visit, they would bring one of my sisters and brothers with them. At that time, I thought I only had two siblings but I think I found out at some point that I actually had four. Being a young child, I didn't understand this situation at all. My grandparents would announce, "Your mom and dad are coming to visit," but I was confused about who they even were. Early on, I couldn't comprehend that my grandparents were not my parents because one, I lived with them, and two, I didn't see my parents that frequently.

I cannot recall how often I did see my parents but once I realized who they were, I would cry to go home with them. I simply did not understand why – if they were my parents – I didn't live with them and my siblings. Nor did I understand how they could just leave me after every visit. I felt as if my own mother and father did not want me and would often cry out loud with my sweet grandmother consoling me. She'd assure me of my parents' love and explain that they just didn't have a place for me right then. At times I would get so angry at them, I'd run off and hide instead of hugging them goodbye when they left. Of course, none of this meant I didn't love my grandparents – I most certainly did – but try explaining something like that to a 6-year-old. A child that age just doesn't get it. And while I do have some fond memories of my parents during this time, I think it is mostly from seven- to- eight years old.

If you could have seen my mom in those days, she was an exceptionally pretty lady with an abundance of beautiful hair and perfectly applied make-up. I doubt there was ever a time when I didn't see her dressed to the nines. I used to wonder, *why can't I look like her?* Even though my mom was attractive, she was a tough lady whom my uncles enjoyed teasing; teasing her was kind of like teasing a bull in a china cabinet. She was the type of woman who was a sight for sore eyes but hell to tangle with. She had plenty of sass and a mean punch to go with it. Back then I wanted to be just like her, wearing feminine dresses and styling my hair as elegantly as hers. Well, my wishes came true, although I had to wait until my twenties before I started to look like her. Presently I still favor my dad but there are times in which you can really see the resemblance to my mother. Thanks to her influence, my personal appearance is something I learned to appreciate over the years, and to this day, I love to dress nicely.

I was a little older by the time I got to know my older sister and brother and the thing I remember most is that my sister Sharon could sing beautifully. I especially loved it when she sang church hymns like *Precious Lord* or *Amazing Grace* so softly she sounded like an angel. Because these were my mom's favorites, my sister sang them often. My mom sang too though her voice was nothing like my sister's.

This one year, my parents took me and a few others to the York Fair in York County, Pennsylvania. My mom had an unusual love for snakes while my dad was just the opposite – he hated them. So of course, the first stop was the snake pit where my mother immediately picked up a big snake and put it around her neck pretending to wear it like a shawl. Since I wasn't afraid of snakes either, I thought it was a pretty cool thing for her to do, but my dad chided her for being crazy and warned her not to go anywhere near him.

The next stop was a show featuring a woman who supposedly transformed into a gorilla. When they asked if I wanted to go in, I didn't hesitate and my dad put me up on his shoulders so I could see everything while my mom and aunt stayed more toward the back of the tent. If you have ever been in one of these shows, you know they are super dramatic and employ lights creatively to make the effects work. However, to this day I am not sure how it truly happened because when the lady was in the case, she started changing: you could see the hair sprouting on her legs and spreading up her body which started to change right before our eyes. Then she started shaking the cage and with a loud bang it finally dropped open. It seemed she was headed directly towards us. I cannot tell you exactly how I did it but in a split second, I jumped off of my dad's shoulders and bolted out of the tent. Even though my mom and aunt were running too, I was moving so fast I left them in the dust. My heart was pounding and my eyes clearly revealed that I was scared shitless. My dad came out of the tent laughing his ass off and made fun of us the entire way home. Even to this day, whenever he tells this story my father cracks up. He says that I darn near broke his neck jumping off his shoulders.

Sometimes during the summer, my brother and sister would

come to stay at my grandmother's. One day we got this bright idea to take my bike to the very top of the big hill. This bike did not have any pedals, only the metal part the pedals were supposed to go on. Its brakes were the kind you needed to reverse pedal to use. Since I only had one bike and there were three of us, our bright idea was that I would control the bike, my sister would sit on the seat, and my brother would sit on the handle bars since he was smaller. The goal was to gain enough speed to jump the small stream way down in woods. Now you need to envision the scene because there were three distinct parts comprising our way: the first was a dirt path, the second a grass path at best, and the third a trail leading to the stream. While the stream was fairly narrow, the point was to get the bike airborne – with all of us on it – to the other side of it. I was convinced that we could do this although I'm not sure who talked who into it. In hindsight, it was a bad idea. In fact, it was a *stupid* idea, but we still tried it anyway.

The first hill allowed us to pick up speed but by the time we hit the top of the second hill, we were really flying. Then it was all downhill on stone and grass paths. Believe it or not, I was controlling the bike exceptionally well even with the problems posed by the ruts in the road. I just kept pedaling faster and faster. I forgot to mention that with my brother on the handlebars, I couldn't see where we were going which meant it was his job to guide us. When we got down to the straight away heading directly for the stream, we were moving so fast I knew we would make it. Unfortunately, there were a few factors we failed to take into account. The first was how to get the bike into the air with three of us on it and the second was the big log that was partially sticking up out of the ground.

We definitely did not do a recon before executing this brilliant plan. When we were probably about 100 yards from the stream, my brother started yelling incoherently and moving around as if preparing to jump. While I was screaming at him to be still, I did not see what we were really headed for because I was focused exclusively on jumping the stream. The next thing I knew, we hit something really hard and the impact threw my brother one way and me another. Somehow my sister stayed on the bike. It was like watching a cartoon character because she did not have her hands on the handlebars even though she was flying through the air. Before she could regain control, it was all over: she landed on the far side of the stream on the ground as if riding the bike lying down. Then she began to laugh, holler, and cry simultaneously.

Since I thought she was just laughing, I started laughing too – hard enough that I began crying. It didn't dawn on me that she was actually hurt until minutes later. When I tried to pull the bike off of her, she let out an ear-piercing scream. The metal part that the pedal slides onto was stuck in the side of her foot near the heel. It made a hole that was about an inch wide and maybe two inches deep. I just knew we were going to be in deep trouble if they found out how it really happened. My brother and I carried her back to the house so my grandmother could take care of her. Mom-mom was always so calm and tended to it by pouring alcohol directly into the open wound. Oh, my god, this is *not*, I repeat, *not* the right thing to do in this situation. It's somewhat extreme. But if you have no other disinfectant on hand you tend to use whatever is available. If we thought my sister was screaming before, she was *howling* after that. However, the real problem arose a day or so later when her foot was clearly infected – mainly due to the fact that the metal part that dug into it was rusty. What she really needed was a tetanus shot. I guess you can imagine our mom blew a gasket about the whole situation. Still, we survived.

My mother seemed to be multi-talented. During the years I lived with my parents, she worked outside of the home most of the time – private duty nursing, hospice care, construction, and other types of jobs. I have never known her to shy away from hard work. I remember this one year when she was working construction and doing final prep on new homes. Predictably, she worked with mostly – if not all – men. Sometimes she would even have to be the flagger, which meant being out in the hot sun or bitter cold all day. At the time, I did not appreciate this or even think much about it. But reflecting back upon the 70's and imagining what that experience would have been like for her was not real for me until I entered the military and then later, the business world.

I could only imagine what she went through on that job and how strong she would have had to be to stay in it as long as she did. I remember talking to her about how they treated her and she would simply state that she was just as good as they were. I have to give her credit; she was tough, really tough. I just wish I knew more about her upbringing which I believe would help me understand her better. In my gut, I know there had to have been multiple experiences that made her so distant and cold. Yet ironically, there were times when she could be loving and sweet.

During the years my mother worked outside of the home, she still fixed dinner when she got back. Oftentimes we'd start meal prep but most of the time she would cook. Mom was an excellent cook and a stickler for balanced meals. You would get your meat, vegetable, and starch with bread for dinner. She would also make us eat breakfast every day but regardless of the meal, you could not drink your water, tea, orange juice, or milk until you consumed everything on your plate. She never gave us seconds and would usually serve dessert hours after our meal.

What a contrast with the life I lived at my grandparents' home, where everyone was welcome all the time in spite of their tiny accommodations. Everyone loved to visit Mom-mom and Pop-pop; not so my mother. In fact, not all of my father's brothers would even bother to come over, possibly because my mom was so regimented. She'd give orders like, "You can't eat until I serve dinner," then, "You're going to do it in a certain way."

Back then she was a five o'clock dinner person; dishes had to be washed and dried immediately and any dessert scheduled for that day would be served promptly at seven. My mother planned out her meals for the week every week and did her grocery shopping based on whatever she was fixing. She was also the type that would stock her pantry and freezer for the winter until she needed to restock. Looking back, I believe this was her way of managing her budget and stretching meals to ensure we always had food on our table. This is probably the origin of my tendency to have a fully stocked pantry just in case. I also relied on these skills to make it through really tough times in my adult life. Regardless of my relationship with my mother over the years, I have always admired her strength, determination, and overall drive. I may not have made some of the same choices or taken some of the same actions, but I can say that she did them with good intentions in mind.

My dad was also a hard worker and from what I remember, had one steady job. When I was younger, he worked for a dealership but by the time I turned nine or so, he'd found employment with one of the county school systems in the maintenance shop. Like my great-grandfather, Dad was a strong man. Until the day I left home, he was my confidante. During my tough years, I harbored resentment toward my mom and often wished it was just my father and me living under the same roof. Yes, I know it is a horrible confession to make, but it was definitely true back then. My father became the one I looked up to; all I wanted was for him to be proud of me. A mediator of sorts, I could tell my dad anything but not so my mother. He'd try to smooth things over and keep her under wraps when conflicts escalated. I am not sure how he tolerated my mother's words and actions, but it has shown me that love not only makes you blind, it can also render you helpless. When you love someone the way my father loves my mother, you would rather die than to be without them, regardless of the pain they inflict upon you.

As the primary provider, Dad ensured we had everything we

needed. He'd often bring home toilet paper, paper towels, large jars of food like peanut butter, and cleaning items. I am not sure where they came from, but it helped to make ends meet. The only problem was that when you opened a can of tuna or a jar of peanut butter, you had to be prepared to eat it for days on end because nothing went to waste. Dad would even bring home prunes and my mom would pack our lunch with tuna, chips, and prunes for weeks at a time. Peanut butter was easier because we could pack it in old jars and it would keep. My dad was handy around the house and proficient with mechanical items. I remember this one year the transmission went up in my mom's car; I helped him drop the transmission and replace it with a new one. I liked being his helper and would stay outside as long as he was working in the yard. Since I was strong, I would help him with chopping wood, cutting grass, and doing projects outside the house. Unlike my younger brother, who would often escape his chores and never even bother to clean his own room, I was a workhorse. My dad would often give me money in exchange for my help, which I would use it to buy the personal items I needed.

There are countless aspects of my childhood that I cherish and hold dear; these are the experiences that helped to shape who I am today. My love of the Christmas Season and all of its festivities is a direct correlation to the serenity and joy I experienced around this "most wonderful time of year." Invariably, Mom was always happier and even spoke to family members she normally shunned from January through November. For me, Christmas was truly magical because it was one of the rare times in my adolescence when I felt as if we were a family.

Of course, this didn't mean my mother lost any of her idiosyncrasies. Her obsessive-compulsive tendencies meant that everything had to be absolutely perfect – from our Christmas tree trimmings to our professionally wrapped presents. Mom took pride in every little detail; for example, if there were too many ornaments in a row or if the tinsel wasn't delicately placed one strand at a time among the branches, we had to remedy the problem immediately. Still, she didn't go overboard with presents: we each received about five- to- six gifts apiece but there was a specific protocol we had to follow before opening them. One year, I remember my sister and I each received a furnished dollhouse – minus the dolls.

What a difference from the Christmases I'd spent with my grandparents where we'd have to go into the woods to chop down our tree and then place it outside in front of the window after dressing it up with those fat, old-fashioned multi-colored lights and ornaments made from cans!

Today I go all out for the holidays. Although my immediate family comprises just my husband and two daughters, I married into a large family that values the same things I cherished growing up. I love being surrounded by family members and getting together often because we want to – not just for special occasions. During my younger years, my grandmother's home was the meeting place; as an adult, I experience this same sense of belonging when we all gather at my sister-in-law's house most every Sunday. While this present-day ritual does not bring my grandparents back, it fills a void and makes me feel complete.

I have raised our daughters to cherish each other and our extended family because, at various points in my life, this was not always the case for me. My relationship with my daughters is unlike anything I ever had with my own mother. I make a genuine effort to consistently be there for them and remain non-critical even if I don't always agree with their choices. I consider myself not only their mother but their best friend and a shoulder to cry on when they need one. While many things influenced me both positively and negatively during my childhood and adolescence, I only wish I could have fully understood the reason for some of my circumstances, specifically my relationship with my own mother.

While I did not understand my feelings then, I clearly understand them now. I know without a doubt that my mother loved us in her own way. Although I wish we could have been closer over the years, I also realize that nurturing is not her nature. She raised me in the best way she knew how, and for that I thank her. Things may not have been as she planned either; however, life is all about choices. I can tell you that I have chosen to take the best parts of my childhood and use them as the basis for the woman, wife, and mother I am today. My grandmother, my mother, and all of my aunts were working women regardless of the type of work. They took care of their households, raised their families, and still found time to share with others. In hindsight, I am thankful my life was filled with plenty of strong women who have helped me to understand the power that influence – both positive and negative – can have in shaping the choices we make in our own adult lives.

CHAPTER 3

LOSING YOU - DEALING WITH DISAPPOINTMENT, ANGER, AND DEATH

As human beings, many of us hold cherished memories of loved ones we've lost. Does the inevitable experience of death become easier with every person you lose? Does knowing what to expect somehow make it less sorrowful? In my experience, there are times when you feel as if your insides are being ripped apart and times when you believe you will go crazy from grief.

I was a young girl of about six or seven the first time I dealt with losing someone I loved: my great-grandmother, the woman I called "Grandma." My memories of her are jumbled into a few years but I believe she lived until her 70s or possibly even older. Even with vague recollections, there are a few important qualities about her that stand out in my mind including her adherence to an unchanging daily routine. She would awaken every morning, wash up with a basin of water, get dressed, and go downstairs for breakfast. It seemed she'd consistently eat poached eggs, toast, and grapefruit accompanied by a cup of coffee. Like most women of her generation, my great- grandmother wore dresses every day, along with thick stockings held up with rubber ties. As I mentioned before, her hairstyle consisted of four snow white braids pinned to her head.

After finishing breakfast, Grandma would take her morning walk around the yard. This was her routine every single day without fail; that is, until the one morning when she did not want to get out of bed. Mom-mom went to check on her and immediately knew something was wrong. While I don't remember if the doctor made a house call or if they took Grandma to his office, I do recall my parents coming to the house. As soon as they arrived my mother headed upstairs to tend to her. The family was called in around the same time but I was forbidden to even go up to the second floor. I don't recall exactly how long she lingered between life and death but it was long enough for one of my uncles to get home in time from Germany, where he was serving in the military. It was the tail end of the Vietnam War.

What sticks in my mind about that night was being awakened by my uncle; he stood by the bed and when I realized who it was I sprung straight into his arms. I think he made it home just in time because Grandma passed away soon after. It was bitterly cold outside and the icy roads made it impossible for the Undertaker to get to the house so the boys had to carry her out with a sheet covering her body. They put her in the back of my grandfather's old pickup truck and brought her out to meet the undertaker. I don't remember much beyond that. Although I did not fully understand what had just occurred, the realization that she would not be coming back hit me hard. All I could do was stand at the window and cry. After she died, the house we all lived in – the house my great-grandmother owned – was passed on to my grandmother.

As a child, the concept of death is tough to wrap your head around. Do you remember when you lost your first pet? I do. Even if it wasn't technically my first, it's the one whose death was the most traumatic. We had a menagerie of animals but one, in particular, our dog Coyte, was old and blind. It was amazing how he would wander around without getting into anything harmful until one summer day when we were burning the trash pile and the fire was at its peak. I was playing in the yard but not within close proximity. As soon as I heard a dog howling in pain, I ran in the direction of the fire see what was going on. Poor Coyte. He always loved to roll in the grass but this day he rolled too close to the fire. By the time they got to him, his whole backside was engulfed in flames. Up to that point, I had never experienced anything so horrific and I started screaming and crying for them to help him. I don't remember much after that except that he was gone. I do recall going back to look at the fire and could not get the gut-wrenching image of his enflamed body out of my mind. No one, especially a young child, should have to experience such a gruesome site – the sickening sounds, smell, and horror of it all.

For many of us, our fears are deeply rooted in our minds based on the events and encounters we deal with from birth to childhood and from adolescence to adulthood. Some of these anxieties don't surface until later in life while others are suppressed forever. After my dog essentially incinerated I developed a healthy respect for fire but also a fear of being burned to death, or of watching helplessly as another pet suffered the same fate. Such powerful apprehension can create seemingly insurmountable obstacles and manifest itself in unanticipated ways.

I lost my beloved grandfather when I was around 10 or 11 years old and his death was even more devastating because I believed it was my fault. Why? It happened right after I moved in with my parents. They'd deliberately taken me out of his home when they knew he wouldn't be there, depriving us both of the chance to say goodbye, much to his anger and disappointment. Soon after, he became sick and by the time they discovered it was cancer, he was extremely ill. That was another thing I didn't understand but came to dread, although my grandfather took me aside and explained that he'd have to go away for treatment. Various family members took turns driving him to the Veterans Hospital in Martinsburg, West Virginia, where he underwent the cancer-killing therapies used to fight the disease at that time. Some days he would return in horrible pain accompanied by overwhelming nausea. It was hard to watch a man of his stature go through such an ordeal. I would hug him, rub his head, and assure him it would be alright but on the inside, I was incredibly scared and knew that whatever disease he had was worse than I could possibly imagine.

There were moments when we would not go into the house or make any noise because he was struggling so badly. I could not help but think it was all my fault; if I hadn't left he never would have gotten sick in the first place. There were days when he would just cry, hold his hands to his head and shake. I'm not sure if a serious disease like cancer is harder on the patient or the people who love them: for me, knowing there was absolutely nothing I could do to help my grandfather was painful and frustrating. I don't remember how long his suffering went on, but I do recall the day they took him back to Martinsburg for what turned out to be his final trip. He'd requested to go back because he did not want to be home during Easter, knowing he couldn't handle the visitors. I believe it was his way of trying to ease the burden on my grandmother. I'm pretty sure my father had driven him to the hospital and by the time he returned to the house my grandfather's condition had taken a turn for the worse. Funny, deep inside I knew that would be the last time I'd see him on this earth. Even when I accepted the fact that my grandfather's cancer diagnosis was not caused by my leaving, it didn't matter. I was still devastated. I also knew that cancer was a disease I never wanted to get.

This "C monster" seemed to plague our family tree. In one family alone we lost five people to it in one form or another. But although I grieved all family deaths regardless of the cause, the ones who succumbed to cancer forced me to relive every other cancer death every time I looked into their eyes. One particular loss from cancer tugs at my heartstrings the most: my beloved grandmother.

Mom-mom was one of the kindest, most loving human beings you could ever meet – strong-minded as well as able-bodied. After my grandfather had passed, she carried on and kept the family together. I cared for her so deeply I wanted her to come to live with us after I gave birth to my second daughter. She was diagnosed when I was in officer candidate school (something I'll discuss in more detail a little later).

When she went in for treatment that Friday evening, I was scheduled to attend our training weekend. I had talked to her on the phone the day before and promised to come see her before I had to report. I recall walking into her room and noticing she was doing okay if a bit weak. When I offered to stay with her and cancel my plans, she refused. I remained with her as long as I possibly could before she reprimanded me to get going. Leaving her was especially difficult because it brought back memories of how I felt when forced to leave Pop-pop. I cried all the way to the training and as soon as I arrived I met with the tactical officers to tell them I was quitting, even though Mom-mom reassured me she'd be alright. And she was, for the most part.

The following months were rough on her but she made it through all of the treatment, which thankfully put the cancer into remission. Almost to the day a year later they found another lump; apparently the cancer had spread. It was around the time I was getting married that she embarked upon another round of cancer-fighting protocols. On the day of my wedding, she was not feeling well enough to attend – a huge disappointment because of all the people I wanted there, Mom-mom topped the list. A month later, I got pregnant with my new husband's and my first child, my second daughter. When I shared the joyous news with my grandmother, I invited her to come live with us and her great-grandbaby, hoping this would lift her spirits and inspire her to beat the cancer again.

But she shook her head and told me she most likely wouldn't be around to see this one. I, of course, replied that she should stop speaking such nonsense; she had plenty more time to spend here on this earth. My grandmother stated plainly that even though she was tough, she didn't have the strength to overcome this time around. Then she promised she would always be my guardian angel.

Sadly, she was correct: I found out I was pregnant in August of 1992 and Mom-mom joined Pop-pop in heaven in November of that same year. For almost four months, I cried at different points throughout every day. I would talk to her like I did when she was alive and at times I even smelled her near me. While skeptics may attribute this to a grieving mind playing tricks or an overactive imagination, I don't believe that. Even to this day, I miss her dearly. I don't smell her anymore, which means she has moved on.

Simultaneously, I was getting to know my new mother-in-law whom I'd met for the first time when my husband and I were dating, and the second time on our wedding day. Did I mention I married into an Indian family? Regardless, my mother-in-law always treated me with class and dignity even though I am probably not the woman she would have chosen for her youngest son. Still, she always respected me. When she stayed with us for the wedding, she would fix me tea and crackers when I came home from work – something unheard of in my time. Though quite unexpected her thoughtful deeds were very much appreciated. I grew to love and respect her unrelentingly. She was strong – and I loved strong women. In her words and actions, she consistently demonstrated to me why she was who she was and that alone commanded my respect. When she left us to return to Trinidad, I promised I would take good care of her baby, her son. She began to cry; I knew I'd been given one of her most precious jewels and I treated him accordingly. My sweet mother-in-law did not live to witness the birth of our child; she passed away three weeks before I was scheduled to have a cesarean. I was devastated because I could not attend her funeral and support my husband and father-in-law during this difficult time. But at a month out my doctor had shut down all travel.

I had to make it almost up to the point of delivery before my husband would be back home. I thought I was being cheated: my grandmother was taken from me in the fall and my mother-in-law in the spring. I had a hard time dealing with the losses but knew I had to be strong for his family and mine. These amazing women had so much in common I believe they were both destined to be in my life for a prescribed amount of time. Their purpose was to show me the similarities within the differences between two women from two divergent places, cultures, and times. My friends had warned me not to marry my husband because of the cultural disparities but I knew better. It was right; this match was simply meant to be. My grandmother knew it also and advised me to follow my heart. She told me the story of her and Pop-pop – a story that has much in common with my in-laws, notwithstanding the contrasting locations and customs. They were both tough women: one promised and one given. What is the true difference? As far as I'm concerned they were both heaven-sent, a gift from God. That is not luck but destiny. After these experiences, I lost more loved ones to cancer and knew that somewhere in my *grand plan* this C monster would rear its ugly head again.

Forgetting to Smile

In my early years, it seemed I was always happy and smiled most of the time. My grandparents, uncles, and aunts always praised me and made me feel incredibly special. I was a good kid though maybe a bit spoiled by my grandparents. While I had a temper, I was not disrespectful or disobedient; I didn't have a smart mouth and I clearly understood the difference between right and wrong. I also knew how to treat others with respect unless they were individuals who gave me no choice but to negatively engage. However, starting around the fifth grade, I would often get into fights or arguments and found I was falling into a pattern of wanting to be somewhere – *anywhere* – else. Some of that was due to the adjustment of living with my parents and siblings after nine years of living with my grandparents and not having to deal with my immediate family on a daily basis.

For any child at any age, this would be a huge transition to make but at nine years old, the role a mother plays in a girl's life is especially significant. Many would argue that a mother is crucial at every stage of childhood and adolescence but I think there are ages when that mother-daughter connection is extremely fragile. As a girl, your mother is the one person with whom you long for a close relationship. Because I had such a meaningful, affectionate relationship with my grandmother, having an emotionally detached mother impacted me more than I realized.

Some folks hold themselves hostage to the negative experiences they've been exposed to in childhood for their entire lives. Even well into adulthood, they do not or cannot seem to shake the habit of constantly criticizing, insulting, nagging, or just being mean to another person. Perhaps in their minds this kind of behavior is normal based on what they've seen, heard, and endured from an early age; they've unconsciously internalized unhealthy human interactions and accepted them as the norm. In my mother's case, she had an uncanny ability to make you feel as if you were constantly being scrutinized under the microscope of judgment.

Living under her roof, I always felt wrong, bad, not good enough, or worthless. I didn't know how to handle it at all, having been plucked out of the warm, loving environment of my grandparents' home. Worse, my mother's harsh words, put-downs, and criticisms would come at such unexpected times I felt like I was constantly walking on eggshells. The actions I'd originally associated with praise would now incite anger expressed as yelling or chastisement. Call me naïve or clueless, but we did not treat each other this way when I lived under my grandparents' roof. There, we had clearly defined rules and expectations for how we treated one another – and calling anyone lazy or stupid, or attacking their skin color for being "yellow" was completely unacceptable. My mother called me names I'd never even think of calling my own children.

My coping mechanism manifested in fear and detachment. I was afraid to even say anything or to look at my mother close-up, and I internalized my unhappiness by shutting myself off. Every part of me yearned to be back with my grandparents but I didn't dare bring it up, except with my siblings in whispers when we were alone in our rooms. Sometimes my mother would overhear us and demand to know what we were whispering about, her attention, of course, focused on me. Other times I'd simply stay in my room until we could go outside or head off to school. Since I was never once told what I was doing wrong or made to understand how my actions might have been unacceptable to her, it was impossible to make corrections. I was a kid in a no-win situation.

At some point, my sister and I started talking about running away from home. While we had different reasons, we shared the same goal: to get as far away as we could. But although we attempted to escape several times, we were always caught. Keep in mind, we lived in the country and had to walk miles and miles to get anywhere. On some occasions, we'd sleep outside in the fields not really knowing where we were headed. Looking back, we were probably hoping to get to Washington DC but the farthest we ever got was Olney, Maryland. For me, school was a safe haven; however, it was also the place where I portrayed myself as a tough girl in order to vent my frustrations or express my belligerence when it suited the purpose. Somewhere along the way, I lost my inner self and my outer smile. I'm not suggesting I never smiled in those days, just that I rarely had reason to do so.

Anger and Alcohol

Undoubtedly, many families have their disputes in addition to their good times and not-so-good times. The difference for me is that while living with my grandparents during my formative years, I never once heard them argue. Ever respectful, Pop-pop never raised his hand or voice to Mom-mom. One day I recall two of the boys fighting – or at least, that was my perception. It upset me so much I jumped on one of my uncle's backs and proceeded to bite him, crying and shouting at them because I wanted them to be nice to each other.

By contrast, my parents seemed to have a tumultuous relationship. While I never fully understood the underlying cause of their rough patches, they mainly occurred when alcohol was involved. The discord in the home was not limited to the two of them: there always seemed to be some kind of negative undercurrent with every relationship. The most frequent family feuds took place between my mother and another family member. I never understood what sparked them, nor did I ever understand why they happened in the first place. All I knew was that I wanted everyone to co-exist peacefully. When you're a child, it's easy to take this perspective because the people you love can do no wrong.

On occasion, my mother's conflicts with other people would extend to neighbors, aunts or uncles, and even my grandmother. Every time there was a problem between my mother and grandmother, Mom would forbid us to visit even though we could look out our kitchen window and see our grandmother's house. From my child's point of view, this situation was unfamiliar and abnormal. I am not sure how to explain the confusion or anger I felt as a result: I began to believe that if not for me, there would be harmony in the family. Often, my mother would look at me with scorn and tell me I was just like them – them being my dad's side of the family. Other times, Mom would lash out at all of us kids or someone else entirely. Sadly, we began to look forward to her "drinking days" because alcohol transformed her into someone we could actually talk to. On these days, which normally took place over a weekend, she would at times open up and behave like the loving person who seemed to be buried deep within her. Whenever she drank excessively, she'd forget her contempt for my father's family and invite them over. But there were also plenty of times when you just wanted to be invisible and out of her line of focus.

While this may come across as a harsh view to others, these are my memories of what I felt and perceived as a child. I cannot speak for my siblings because their perspective and circumstances differed from mine: they'd been with my mother from birth and I had not. I'd spent my early years in a home that was rich in love, even if poor in material comforts and even some of the basic necessities of life we take for granted. Now I found myself living in a house that in all outer appearances had everything a child could want – except consistency in affection, respect, and other expressions of love.

On one of my mother's "good" days, she invited my grandmother to come up for a drink. We were excited by the prospect of this unexpected gesture, believing it could be the first step in ending all of the rancor and in paving the way for us to see Mom-mom regularly. While our grandmother visited with our mother, we decided to go down to her house to hang out with Sissie. Since it was a short walk away, we could easily go back and forth and get our fill of the wonderful old home. Little did we know but later that evening our hopes of reconciliation would be dashed. When we arrived back at the house, we heard my mother calling my grandmother names I wouldn't even utter to a stranger. Then Mom yelled at her to "get out."

What happened?

Earlier in the day, everything seemed to be fine. Somewhere

along the way, the mood changed although I never did find out what actually transpired between them. You're probably wondering what my father was doing, but I as I recall he made an effort to diffuse the situation and calm them both down, with no success. Once ordered to leave, my grandmother obeyed and went outside. Evidently unsatisfied, my mother continued to hurl insults as she followed her out to the road, where the nasty interchange continued.

My father did his best to calm my mother down but before we knew it and right before our eyes she reached out, put her hands around Mom-mom's neck, and proceeded to choke her. As my mother shoved my grandmother to the ground, she continued yelling hateful names at her. In his efforts to break it up, Dad repeated, "Mom, get out of here," and "Mom, go home."

The entire incident ignited all kinds of conflicting emotions in me. First and foremost, I was mad because I knew my mother's behavior was unacceptable; she should never have treated my grandmother with such contempt. But I also knew that from this point on I'd be forced to take sides while my right to visit my grandmother at her house was revoked. A short-lived privilege, it seemed.

Furthermore, I realized I'd I also be chastised because my mother associated me with my father's side – the branch of the family she disdainfully referred to as "them." No matter what, she would never totally accept me because she didn't raise me in my early years. But why was she holding me accountable for a decision I didn't even make? Living with my grandparents from birth through nine years hadn't been *my* choice, but *hers*. At three-months-old I was incapable of choosing anything, nor did I possess the awareness to protest a decision made by my parents on my behalf. Don't get me wrong; I believe I got the better deal. However, that didn't excuse her from holding me responsible.

Witnessing my mother abuse my grandmother verbally and physically helped me to understand the power alcohol can hold over an individual. It also helped me to realize it's impossible to determine who or what alcohol – when given full authority – can transform a person into. In the years following this ugly incident, I struggled with my feelings about drinking and started to believe if I became an alcoholic like my mother, then maybe I would "get it." That's when I began to experiment by taking sips of her drinks when she asked me to make them, or whenever she left them untouched at the end of the night.

Mad at the World

After several years of observing these behaviors, it became the norm. I never stopped wondering how my life would have unfolded if I'd been given the opportunity to stay with my grandparents. What if my parents had moved to another county? How much better off would I have been? I hate to admit it because I know it sounds awful but I would constantly dream of either going back to that tiny four-room house, living with one of my other relatives or moving in with someone else altogether. It didn't matter where, I just wanted to be someplace else. I'm sure for some, living in a home filled with modern conveniences would have compensated for having to deal with an emotionally detached mother and an enabling father. But not for me.

The problem with fantasizing is that it only offers a temporary reprieve no matter how often you indulge. In my case, it was only a matter of time between daydreams before the next incident would further erode my self-esteem and force me to question my own worthiness. As human beings and especially young adolescents, our environment inevitably begins to influence our every waking thought and make us wonder if we have the strength to endure another day.

True, I experienced both good and bad days when I lived with my parents. However, the bad days were indescribably awful. Most of the time I'd walk around without much of an expression on my face, fearful my mother would notice and accuse me of having "an attitude." In those instances, she'd yell, "Why are you always poking your lips out? Your face is going to stay that way!" Was it any wonder I avoided talking to her whenever possible? I refused to even look at her unless she was speaking directly to me but even then she'd call me on the carpet due to my mere presence. Consequently, my attitude began to get worse and I developed a chip on my shoulder that seemed to come out of nowhere.

I think I was in the 5th grade when I had my first school fight with one of the boys who used to pick on me occasionally. Even though he was bigger, one day I simply decided to let my anger loose on him and needless to say, I held my own to the point where some would say I taught him a lesson. However, I hadn't anticipated that he would bring his big sister to school the next day in retaliation. Luckily she was all talk: in spite of my bravado, I'm not sure I was prepared to take her on but I didn't back down either. The adrenaline rush shooting through my body was too much to handle, making me feel overwhelmingly jittery and sweaty. The reason I relate this story is that it started me down the track of refusing to take any shit from anyone. After holding my own with the big girl, I had earned a level of respect – and maybe even a certain amount fear – from the other kids, especially the girls. This experience taught me that by being tough, rough, and just downright mean, I could make someone else feel the way I often did when dealing with my mother.

Of course, I didn't consciously acknowledge the underlying motivation for my behavior; I was too young to understand. But looking back on the experience as an adult, I realize that the 5th-grade version of me was mimicking the behavior I saw at home because it made me feel good to hurt someone else in the same manner. I held onto this outlook even into high school: if you were unlucky enough to get on my bad side you became a target, and if you decided to pick a fight with me I would not back down – whether you were a boy or a girl. Conversely, I protected my friends and ensured that no one bothered them. I can admit now that I was somewhat of a bully but only to some people. I did not get into fights often but if provoked, I was always up for the challenge.

On the last day of school one year when I believe I was in the 7th grade, I decided to get back at a few people. One of them was a girl with whom I'd been friends earlier in the year but by semester's end had become an enemy; naturally, I had something in store for her. In an effort to be cool, I'd communicated my plans to the supposedly cool folks on my bus. Just as the bus arrived at school, I moved to the front, holding two raw eggs in my hand. When she boarded, I slapped her in the head with them while everyone began to make fun of her. To this day, I feel horrible about what I did. In fact, she had been a good friend to me but for some reason, I had to be *Miss Big Girl* and humiliate her.

But that's not the end of the story. The same boy and his sister whom I fought in the 5th grade also attended the same school, so I went in search of her. All throughout the day, I threatened her, building up the anticipation of a showdown for our classmates on the last day of school. For me, it was a means of making my mark for the next school year.

Furthermore, since it was a half-day we had plenty of free time to clean out lockers, turn in books, and engage in the customary activities of last day of school. This abundance of time also created the perfect opportunity for a final showdown. Right before the bell was scheduled to ring and release us for the summer, I was walking through the hall with some friends while she was walking in our direction with hers. Just before we reached each other, my friends shoved me at her; because so much tension had already been built up, we immediately started pushing, name-calling and bragging about who was going to kick whose ass.

Well, I refused to let her have the upper hand; therefore, my temper got the best of me and I punched her first. We went at it but this was no ordinary "girl fight;" the two of us were throwing punches. Having grown up around several boys, I applied everything I'd learned, including how to box. Yet all it took was for her to punch me in the face to make me lose total awareness and the next thing I knew a teacher was pulling me off of her. It was not good. They took me to the principal's office where they suspended me for the first five days of the following school year. They also informed me there would be a mandatory parent conference.

This was definitely a bad outcome although I successfully hid the suspension letters for a while. However, it hadn't occurred to me that they would send one later that summer, right before school re-opened. Of course, that was the one letter I didn't intercept. Ultimately I did survive the punishment inflicted upon me by my mother who screamed at me and told my dad about everything I'd done. Although I'll admit I deserved this punishment, it still wasn't as bad as I anticipated.

While I haven't really gotten into fist fights since high school, in my early adulthood years I was always very hot-tempered. Before the words flew out of my mouth, I didn't stop to think about what I was saying or how it would affect someone. If they gave me the slightest reason to get angry, I wasn't very forgiving or ladylike. Eventually, I got into fewer and fewer encounters, but I struggled to control my temper for a long time.

As you might imagine, a hot temper could pose quite a problem in my personal and professional life. One particularly horrendous incident occurred in the workplace stands out in my mind. I was employed in a corporate job and for whatever reason I really disliked this one co-worker, a woman who worked on my team.

From what I can remember, she treated me as if I was beneath her and unworthy of participating in her group. I don't remember what lead to the office confrontation but I should have been disciplined – maybe both of us should have been. Even now, when I think back on my actions that day as I often do, I am appalled by my behavior. I called her names and pushed her as she walked by me. If I knew where she was today, I would apologize for my immaturity and lack of professionalism. What's even worse is that the guys at the office egged me on because they wanted it to happen. Let's just say workplace rules have changed for the better and incidents like these now have serious consequences. In fact, I'm so ashamed of my young adult behavior I no longer tolerate disrespect anywhere.

Finding My Strength In Officer Candidate School

In 1989, my first sergeant and section lead convinced me I possessed excellent leadership skills and needed to become an officer. After much introspection and debate, my exhilaration over the thought of developing myself further won out over fear. Thus, I decided to attend officer candidate school in the National Guard, transferring there in December of 1989 from the Army Reserve. I started the prep session in February of 1990, but it was just the beginning. I wasn't sure exactly what I'd gotten myself into but I knew it formed another vital step in my path to leadership.

During my final phase of officer candidate school, we spent a lot of time maneuvering through the woods of Cumberland, a town located in western Maryland. As a kid, I used to spend all day in the woods hiking and playing and I was definitely in my element. I have always found solace in wooded areas and even being dead-tired and carrying a load of equipment and a weapon, I was basking in the moment. Throughout the two weeks, each team member was assigned various command and staff positions. During this period, we didn't have much time for basic activities like showering;

therefore, when the opportunity presented itself, washing up at the sink and cleaning ourselves with baby wipes turned out to be the most expedient method of personal hygiene. Baby wipes are great because you can use them anywhere for a quick cleansing. Who would have ever thought that learning how to bathe with a tiny amount of water as a child would come in handy as an adult in the military? Quite funny and ironic.

After traveling about five kilometers through steep terrain, we took a brief break alongside one of the ridge tops to eat our MREs. After about 20 minutes it was time to move again. We had to traverse another two kilometers in order to reach the lodge where we would have classroom sessions for the rest of the afternoon. Since our current leadership team had been in place for the last day, we knew a switch was imminent.

Upon arriving at the lodge, we grounded our gear and attended class until 2100 hours that evening – at the absolute worst time. We smelled, we were tired and we had to fight off the "Zzz" monster because if you were caught sleeping, you were likely to be dropped for pushups or some other equally arduous form of physical punishment. Whenever you could feel that monster attacking, it was best to just stand in the back of the room. One thing you quickly learn about sleep deprivation with its accompanying mental and physical stress is that you can develop an ability to sleep almost anywhere – even standing up.

Once we left class that evening, the TAC officers called out the new leadership assignment and gave us 10 minutes to synch up and organize for our move to that evening's site. After receiving instructions to go back to the same place where we'd eaten lunch earlier that day, we were disheartened: none of us had paid attention to the location as instructed. We were always supposed to be aware of our surroundings and remain vigilant and attentive – easier said than done when you are utterly drained. Being assigned the commander spot, I was responsible for getting all 26 of us back to that designated site. Wouldn't you know it, on this particular night there was absolutely no illumination from the moon and the glow in the dark markers on the back of our Kevlar's could not be seen more than five paces from one another?

They took us by truck to the road closest to the site, which meant we had less than one kilometer to go to reach our destination. The biggest challenge in these types of circumstances is making it safely to the location, not losing anyone, and setting up security and the perimeter, with the knowledge that the opposing forces would attack either that night or early in the morning. We quickly formulated a plan: I took 10 candidates with me on the trek back to the location and left a team in place to clear and secure the site to receive the entire team. The remaining candidates were to stay with my deputy and hold in place until we came back and led them in.

Now keep in mind it was pitch dark. Because part of our mission involved practicing noise and light discipline, we couldn't talk loudly or use our flashlights except when necessary to read our maps. My deputy's job was to count off to himself the people leaving, then count the rest to ensure that *only* those 10 had left. Well, as the saying goes, the best-laid plans never seem to turn out. He obviously hadn't understood his role because I returned to discover 11 candidates instead of the 16 who should have remained. Worse, no one even knew when the missing candidates left or what direction they were headed.

As I'm sure you can imagine, I totally lost it. No words could adequately describe the fear and anger pulsating throughout my entire body at that moment. Not far away from our location were several cliffs; thoughts of someone walking right off, getting stuck on one, or worse – sustaining a severe injury, permeated my mind. If ever I have felt like panicking, it was definitely one of those times, yet somehow I managed to keep it together and rely on my leadership skills. Although my main concern was not knowing where five of my candidates were wandering in the woods, my first priority had to be getting the rest of them to safety. Once we got everyone to the site and were preparing to launch the search party, the five candidates showed up. What had made a bad situation, even more, distressing was that the security team had seen them go by but mistakenly thought they were the opposing force. Therefore, they laid low without making any sound or movement. Only when everyone was bedded down and security teams assigned for the night was I able to get some rest. Early the next morning, we conducted security watch and heard the opposing force searching for us. Believe it or not, they couldn't find us, mainly because our location was about 200 yards east of where we were originally supposed to set up, which meant they passed us without even knowing.

Although a significant amount of years had not transpired between my appalling workplace behavior and this officer candidate event, there was a dramatic difference in the way I responded. Along the way, I'd been involved in lesser altercations both in office environments and in my personal life, which made me realize I had to take control of my behavior. Things needed to change. That night in the woods, the new and improved me stepped up when I needed her the most. I understood the utmost importance of teamwork, and that being part of the team does not always entail being the center of negative attention. Throughout these years, people who genuinely cared about me arrived in my life. And I know without a doubt they made a difference.

Coping with Loss in the Military

I don't think anything can ever prepare you for losing a loved one to death. It seems no matter how many times it happens, the reaction and feelings are the same. During my time as a commander of a maintenance company, I experienced my first non-battle losses.

They all stand out prominently in my memory but none more than the very first, possibly because it hit so close to home. One of my soldiers – a jovial person who loved to joke around constantly – approached me to request a meeting with my first sergeant and me. We set it up for the same day, never expecting to hear the devastating news he shared with us about his cancer diagnosis, which gave him less than a year to live. Of all the possible discussion topics that had floated through my mind, cancer had not been one of them.

As we talked about his illness, conflicting emotions consumed me. Having already lost two family members to the C monster, I knew he had a tough battle ahead of him; I also knew that he, his family, and my soldiers needed my support. Good or bad, I'd been through this with my grandparents and had some knowledge of what to expect. He asked that we continue to allow him to serve and that we not treat him any differently. He also wanted to remain a part of the team's scheduled overseas training mission, inquiring if that was still permissible. I kept my composure during the whole discussion but once he left the office, I broke down in tears. Perhaps it wasn't the appropriate thing to do but it seemed only fitting. Contemplating the pain and discomfort, he would have to endure and its impact on his family tore at my heart. I didn't even know if I could look at him month after month and act as if things were normal when in fact they were anything but.

However, as the summer progressed it was amazing to watch him deal with his illness. He really did act as if nothing was wrong; he carried on as normal except on days when he truly didn't feel well. However, this one day his section lead approached me right after one of their field support missions to inform me that even though things appeared to be status quo, our soldier was struggling with terrible pain. He then proceeded to tell me I had to break the news that he would not be able to participate in the overseas mission. We both agreed it was much too risky; he would not handle the travel well. If memory serves, we had a hard time convincing him. My every intention had been to allow him to go on what would most likely be his last mission: I wanted it to be as unforgettable as possible. Unfortunately, the risk was too great and I had to deny him the opportunity. Though upset, he understood. When the mission time came around, he was too sick to go anyway; by then, his health had definitely started to spiral downward and all I could do was pray he could hang on until they returned. I made sure he knew when the team arrived at their location and when they were coming home. The day after the they returned, he passed away. I'll never forget the words his wife spoke to me during his viewing: "Ma'am, he was waiting for them to get back before he decided to go."

No matter how many times you've had to say goodbye to a loved one, it is never easy. Trying to fill the emptiness inside and figure out how to carry on is something I have struggled with in the aftermath of every loss. You just have to realize you can find strength and comfort by celebrating the lives of your loved ones daily, even after they're gone. Reminiscing and talking about the joy they've given me while they were alive is one of the many ways in which I cope with this inevitability. While some may believe crying is a sign of weakness, to me it is a sign of strength and resolution. It helps me to put things in the right place in my heart and I find it is easier and healthier to let those feelings out instead of bottling them up inside.

CHAPTER 4

BOY TROUBLE – A MATTER OF SELF-WORTH AND SELF-ESTEEM

My interest in boys began when I was in the seventh grade. However, at that time, I wasn't exactly the image most boys held in their minds of the perfect "girly girl." Not only did I have a boyish figure without nice curves, but my hairstyle also left much to be desired, as did my wardrobe. Although I was mainly attracted to the jocks, their interest was mostly directed toward the cheerleaders or pom-pom girls. I was neither.

Adding to my problems, most of my classmates lived near each other in a defined area while I lived way out in the woods. In those days, we didn't have technologies like Skype or cell phones with unlimited calling plans; therefore, making long distance calls could easily inflate the phone bill. If I dared to do such a thing, the charges would show up on the bill every month and land me in a heap of trouble. None of us were allowed to call anyone long distance, which meant once I left school for the day I could not speak to my friends on the phone. As you might expect, this created somewhat of a barrier in developing a good social life, adding to the peer pressure I felt about wanting to fit in.

Paradoxically, while I may have behaved like a bully at times I also wanted to fit in. The guys I liked had no interest in me other than as a friend. My clothes, while adequate, weren't stylish. Even worse, my mom insisted on buying bras my sister and I had to share even though we weren't even the same size. Her breasts were much bigger than mine so the bras were always too big for me – which was especially embarrassing when required to change in the locker room in preparation for gym class. When you're a young girl of twelve or thirteen in the throes of burgeoning adolescence, nothing is more dreadful than developing your bust at a much slower pace than everyone else. At that age, I was still tall and thin.

By this point, my hair had broken off, mainly because my mother never supplied the proper products to care for it. What a contrast to my grandmother who'd painstakingly washed and conditioned it for me on a regular basis. Now I hated the way I looked and as I got closer to the ninth grade, I attempted to change my appearance. Like most young girls, I wanted to be pretty. I wanted to have nice hair again, the kind I enjoyed until age nine until it became impossible to maintain on my own. Without the necessary items, it broke off. Thus, I went from having long healthy hair that went down my back to very short, brittle hair. Worse, in a matter of years, I went from thinking I was cute to thinking I was ugly.

My feelings of alienation were exacerbated by the fact that my girlfriends either began to date early or could, at least, hang out with the guys because they all lived nearby. I could do none of that. This, along with a multitude of other factors, influenced the way I felt about myself. Not only did I fail to attract the attention of the boys, sometimes they cruelly teased me. They'd play games where they would pretend to like me only to hurl insults at me. Did they know how devastating that was? Probably not. To hide my pain, I'd often hide behind my "tough girl" exterior. I didn't want to give them the satisfaction of knowing how much they'd hurt me. Playing into my insecurities was my situation at home where my siblings taunted me about my skin color. Mimicking my mother, they would call me "yellow." I know they did not realize how much emotional pain they were inflicting but being forced to move in with them and cope with feelings of not belonging impacted my sense of self-esteem and perceived self-worth. Consequently, it played an enormous role in determining my attitude, behavior, and the way I saw others. At times, I even wished I was white or mixed-race – just anyone other than who I was.

The only place I could feel large and in charge was on the basketball court. Unlike every other aspect of life, in the sports arena I had an abundance of confidence: while basketball was my first love, I knew I excelled at just about every sport. No matter what was going on everywhere else, when I was on the court, all was forgotten. Eventually, I did have boyfriends during high school although in most cases these part-time relationships did not last long. I recall one, in particular, an adorable white guy with a southern drawl whom I dated on and off. I kept our relationship on the "down-low," fairly certain that neither one of us wanted anyone to know about it. He'd moved to our area from down south; we'd met in electronics class and formed a good friendship. Unfortunately, our relationship didn't last. He was a member of the football team and had a thing for one of the cheerleaders so naturally I lost out.

By my tenth grade year, I summoned the courage to call a childhood crush who went to a high school in the New Windsor area. Although he was older than me, I'd had a crush on him from the time I was little. The nephew of one of my dad's brother's wives, we were not biologically related. Since he wasn't long-distance, I could talk to him on the phone, which facilitated our relationship. We dated for a good while – or at least until after his senior prom.

This guy had a job and his own car, which meant he could pick me up and pay for dates. When my aunt, who was also my godmother, passed away he was there for me. She had been happy that we were making a go of it but sadly, it did not last too long and we broke up after prom. He had been fooling around and I was not as interested in trying to make it work. Go figure, after desperately wanting a boyfriend, then getting a good-looking one, I still had serious self-esteem issues. Having a boyfriend did nothing to change my perception of myself. In fact, all the guys seemed to want was to get to home plate; they weren't thinking of anything other than what was between their legs. If you didn't put out, they called you names; if you did put out, they called you names. There was simply no way to win. Boys could be so cruel.

Heading into my early adult years, especially after leaving home in November of 1980, I grappled with the issue of believing I could make something of myself on my own. My mother's vicious words that I would never amount to anything reverberated through my head constantly; try as I might, I couldn't dislodge them. It was as if they'd taken up permanent residence in my mind for the sole purpose of impacting my way of thinking, my relationships with others, and – most importantly – my relationship with me. Regardless of how it was supposed to be, the way my mother treated me left an indelible impression and manifested into issues I had to address for years to come.

A multitude of factors converged to create all of my challenges. While I have no doubt my home situation could have been much worse – I could have lived in an environment in which my parents were into drugs or criminal activity – it doesn't change how I felt. Although as I mentioned before my sister and I tried to run away several times, I ultimately left home as a result of sexual abuse from a family member. I'll discuss the details a little later, but for now, will just note that the incident resulted in a huge argument with my parents, forcing me to leave home. Yes, I wanted to be someplace else, but I certainly didn't want to be homeless without a stable, permanent place to live. That day is forever imprinted in my mind even more so than the sexual abuse inflicted upon me by the family member himself. With the addition of homelessness to my list of negative emotions and experiences, it was almost a perfect storm.

On a positive note, my sister and her foster mother took me in for a little while until her foster mother informed me I had to help pay the rent. They were moving to another place and she wanted a couple of hundred dollars from me in exchange for staying with them, even though a couch was all that she could provide. Nevertheless, I tried to continue going to school, playing basketball, and keeping things as normal as I could. But my situation was anything but normal. My basketball coach, Coach Dawson, picked me up in Frederick and gave me a ride to school. Even though I didn't confide in him about what was really going on, he knew I did not have the best support at home. I was already feeling deprived and scared before I left, but being told by my father that it was time for me to leave created an entirely new dimension of fear for me as a sixteen-year-old. Suddenly I realized I had to get a job just to have lunch money, not to mention personal necessities. I got a job at Burger King but my limited hours barely allowed enough for the basics. My other issue was transportation. I didn't have a car which meant getting to work was a problem since we lived downtown near South Street and the Burger King was located outside of the city limits. In my situation, it might as well have been 30 miles away.

Most days I would either walk or bum a ride to work. Because I ended up being late several times, they told me they were not going to put me on the schedule anymore. I had to find another job and had no idea what I was going to do. But I started looking around and found employment at Bavarian Pretzel in the Francis Scott Key Mall in January of 1981. To make things easier on myself, I also transferred from Linganore High School to Thomas Johnson High School that December. As you might imagine, all of this turmoil created significant obstacles; focusing on school became a problem.

Under the best of circumstances, relocating to a new high school is tough on a teenager; in my case a successful adjustment was impossible. I didn't like my new school or my new classmates, many of whom were the same girls from the rival basketball team who always caused problems for me. I began failing my assignments and tests. In spite of my efforts to hang out with my old friends and my sister's attempts to guide me even while handling her own problems, I just didn't fit in. In March of 1981, near the end of my junior year, I made the decision to drop out of school.

While I hated to do it, I didn't know what else I could do. Leaving school freed up time for me to take on more hours at the pretzel shop and I eventually made enough money to rent a room with an older white couple who had specific rules I had to follow as their second boarder. I don't remember how much the room cost but I managed to make do with what I was earning. I think I stayed with them for at least two months but don't remember exactly. Living there, I had plenty of freedom and could come and go as needed. However, I was not allowed to have company of any kind. As time went on, I made friends in the neighborhood.

Living in Frederick after leaving home, I was able to buy nicer clothes and dress better. But living on my own was tough; sometimes buying something new wasn't an option. I made new friends – girls who were simultaneously tough and feminine. They would help me with my hair and show me different ways to enhance my looks. I don't think they ever knew how much it meant to me and how good it made me feel, but they helped me begin to find that young woman inside.

As I continued to hang out with my friends, I got the idea that finding a new place would be best for my social life. Yes, I was getting too big for my britches to say the least.

Given the hours I was working at my job, I thought I could handle a larger unit. I moved again – this time to a comfortable basement apartment with a kitchen, bathroom, and sleeping area. It was a great place to live for a couple of months; that is, until I couldn't pay rent anymore and came home one day to find an eviction notice. With just days to vacate, one of my friends helped me gather my belongings while another agreed to keep them at her house. Some nights I'd sleep at this friend's house but other nights when I missed curfew I was on my own.

The Martins tried to help me as much as possible but I started to get out of hand because I wanted to run the streets. Much like the saying "Be careful what you wish for," my desire resulted in my living on the streets for a good portion of the summer of 1981. I would sometimes sleep at the shop in the mall, especially if I had to be at work the next morning. Alternately, I stayed with different friends here and there. I started hanging out in the Carver apartment community and around Frederick High School, which became the norm. It also meant that I surrounded myself with tougher friends.

My friends all lived at home and many of them worked. I hated it when people asked me where I lived but I also knew if I wanted to rent a room again, I needed more money. To that end, I called a friend of my sister to ask him if I could borrow some cash. He agreed to my request and set up a place and time to meet with me. When I met him in the parking lot near the mall, he informed me that the only way he'd give me the money was in exchange for sex; in fact, he told me he'd pay me regularly for ongoing sexual favors. It then occurred to me that he essentially wanted me to be a prostitute, *his* prostitute. I also realized that in spite of my desperate need for money, this was definitely not going to happen. Even under these dire circumstances, I had enough respect for myself and my body to reject such a degrading proposition.

What a wake-up call! I already knew I was at the bottom, but until this unfortunate incident, I had no idea I had hit *rock bottom*. After sleeping at the shop for several nights, I knew I had to do something different or else I was headed for a serious train wreck. On one these days of contemplation as I was walking in the mall during a break, I came across the National Guard recruiting display.

I walked right by the first time but on my way back to the pretzel shop I stopped and talked with them. The recruiters convinced me to take the ASVAB (Armed Services Vocational Aptitude Battery) test and consider joining. I agreed and it was probably the best decision I had made since being on my own. I signed the paperwork to join the National Guard in May and was sworn in in June of 1981. May turned out to be a big month, one I truly felt marked my turning point. I also changed jobs and started working at Airpax later in the summer, which paid well. Of course, it was a little too late since I'd be leaving them for basic training in October.

During this period, I continued to stay off and on with the Martins. It was tough because living with some other family that did not have to take me in and trying to abide by their rules did not always work. I had too much freedom prior to this and felt that since I was not a student but a full-time employee I should be able to do what I wanted. What I did not realize was that my attitude was disrespectful to them; it was also setting a bad example for my friend who was about a year younger than me. The Martins sat me down for a long talk and asked me to stay with them as long as I abided by their rules. I tried to stay out of trouble but I desperately needed a wake-up call. Little did I know, I was about to get one at basic training.

I remember the recruiter picking me up from their house, saying my goodbyes, and catching my very first flight ever at Hagerstown Airport, with a final destination of St. Louis Missouri. While I should have been scared shitless, I was feeling as if I was on the top of the world, a *big lady* going away to the military. I landed in St. Louis and was transported to the reception station for processing. After we processed in we were taken by cattle truck to our barracks locations. The drill sergeants started yelling as soon as the doors opened and that big tough lady ran the other way. I was not sure whether to run, scream, or cry but knew it was not the time to be a chicken. I had to put on my big girl panties and just deal with what was ahead for me.

Basic training was full of classroom, practical, and physical training. I was good at the physical part and found it easy to assimilate into the environment. To my delight, I discovered something else in which I excelled, something beyond just basketball and other sports. I also truly enjoyed being challenged. My confidence started growing and my leadership skills started to emerge. I don't remember when it happened but I was assigned as the senior squad leader some weeks into basic training. This meant that I was moved to the squad leader room, a single room, and placed in charge of 40 or so females.

In fact, my training officer used to call me his airborne ranger because one day when he was watching us on the obstacle course I went up the tower of death in record time. He told me to do it again but with the stipulation that I had to beat my previous time. You can bet that I did, trying to show off my tree-climbing skills from my youth, which came in handy. While there were plenty of challenges and aspects about basic training that made me want to run the other way, I enjoyed being counted on to make things happen. I was being paid to train and getting three meals a day, which for the most part was better than I'd had it since leaving home. When the time came to leave basic and head to advanced individual training, I cried as I said my goodbyes to the other ladies and the staff. It was a bittersweet moment but one that I remember to this day. I felt incredible pride and exceptionally good about myself. I wasn't a failure after all; at least, I thought I wasn't.

My next destination was Fort Huachuca in Arizona for Intelligence school while many of the others were going home for the Christmas break. I left basic training in December of 1981 to report to combat area surveillance radar repair school. What I did not realize is that classes would not start until January and many of the people were on break. This meant that there was plenty of time to get into trouble. After being in an environment with seemingly endless restrictions and getting to AIT, it was a stark contrast. My weekends were free while during the week I was assigned to details. One night I went to the post club where we mixed with the permanent party folks, the ones stationed there who have completely finished training. To my shock, the guys in attendance actually showed interest in talking to me. One fateful evening, I danced with a tall, dark, and handsome guy. He was agile on his feet and when he smiled, he lit up the room. Little did I know I would fall head over heels for him.

The charming John Henry Ford III swept me off my feet. After that initial first meeting, we spent all of our free time together when we could. Although I didn't know it at the time, he was scheduled to leave in early February. From my perspective, I thought I was something special because I was dating a permanent party guy. While others warned me about this type of man I did not listen, totally blinded by John's charm and too gullible to realize it. When he left on leave to go home and head to Germany, I felt horrible. He called me almost daily. About midway through his leave, I started to feel physically ill. I was nauseous all the time and got the surprise of my life when I went to sick call to find out what was wrong with me. Here, I was pregnant yet had no clue how it had even happened since I was using contraception.

The doctor informed me that my system had not adjusted from basic training and asked me to think about what I wanted to do. He told me I could get an abortion and continue school, or opt to have the baby since I should finish classes well before labor and delivery. When he inquired if I knew who the father was, I told him of course; I'd only dated one guy since my arrival. I debated about hiding my pregnancy from John but instinctively knew that would not be right. At the same time, I didn't want to abort my child. As hard as I knew this would be, I decided regardless of John's reaction I was having this baby...with or without him.

When I told him, as expected he reacted strongly; I felt as if I had been punched in the stomach. I think we went a few days without talking and I just knew that I was on my own again. Complicating matters was the arduous process of sending and receiving calls. Earlier I mentioned how hard it was to develop and maintain a social life due to my physical distance from my peers and the high cost of long-distance telephone calls. Well, in the United States military prior to the advent of low-cost, internet-based methods of personal communication, the simple act of a phone call between two people required a tremendous amount of effort, the involvement of various people, and the perfect timing. A payphone would ring and whoever happened to be there would answer it, then search the area to see if the intended recipient was anywhere nearby. Forget about any semblance of privacy or convenience. And once you did manage to connect, if the conversation didn't go well, there was no guarantee of rectifying the situation via another phone call.

After John and I had engaged in yet another big argument, I was not expecting him to call me again to propose. Yet that's exactly what happened. I accepted, knowing it would greatly upset my parents but what did they care? It had been months since I'd talked to them and almost a year since I'd seen them. On February 14, 1982, we got married and made plans for me to join him in Germany after I had the baby. However, I could never have predicted the events that would unfold in the following months.

It was a difficult pregnancy. I was sick daily and after about two months, everything began taking a toll on me, along with my course work. I was scheduled to graduate in March of 1982 but failed a test I should have easily passed; as a result, I would have to restart the 10-week program. Since I did not want to hang around for another month waiting for the next course to begin, the National Guard liaison discussed options with me about going to another school. He coordinated with my unit back home and rescheduled me to Fort Benjamin Harrison in Indiana, where I arrived in late February but not without troubles.

After processing, I was put in an open bay barracks, much different from what I had in Arizona. I knew this was not going to work so I consulted with the team to see if I could make other arrangements since I was expecting. The medical staff approved my relocation to a barracks designated for more senior personnel, where I had a private room and bathroom, and a shared kitchen on the same floor. Another big surprise came when I showed up to report for pay for the first time and one of the noncommissioned officers announced that he did not like women in his army...and he damn sure did not like pregnant women. He further explained that if he had any influence over the matter, I wouldn't be there for long. His words shattered my confidence and rocked me to my core: I had never encountered anything like this and he realized he upset me. Adding insult to injury, I had not heard from my new husband in weeks.

This, combined with the other changes, stressed me out even more. One morning after this ugly incident, the school command sergeant major was walking down the hall; I could hear the taps of his shoes on the floor. I tried to keep my face free of expression but knew that if he talked to me, I would lose it. As he walked past me, I greeted him as I normally did whenever I saw him. I fought hard to sound like myself in hopes that he would not notice. But like a good command sergeant major, he not only noticed but saw right through my lackluster, "I am well Command Sergeant Major." When he stopped and came back to where I was standing, he looked at me intently and demanded, "Why are you lying to me?" That was all it took for me to breakdown because I was already hanging by a string. After listening to my troubles with the noncommissioned officer and my heartbreak over a husband who'd seemed to have abandoned me, he assured me everything would be alright. Then he proceeded to address both problems.

Thanks to the efforts of the command sergeant major, the noncommissioned officer was reassigned and did not bother me anymore. He also made contact with my husband's unit and arranged a phone call for me to talk with him. Of course, my husband fed me an excuse about being out in the field and not having a chance to call. To which I replied that mail goes both ways; even if you can't get to a phone as long as your fingers aren't broken, you can write a letter.

While these much-appreciated gestures did not resolve all of my issues, they, at least, helped me to move forward and I graduated at the top of my class. My classmates were absolutely wonderful. Through all of my challenges, they remained my steadfast support, my rock of Gibraltar. After leaving Fort Benjamin, I returned home for the first time in more than a year. Although my parents wanted me to stay with them to have the baby, I knew it was a bad idea. I informed my mom I wanted to move into the city to be close to the hospital. She contacted her cousin Douglass and arranged for me to rent a room from his girlfriend and longtime family friend Phyllis. During this time, Phyllis and I developed a close relationship and I took a job at Frederick High School doing administrative work for the summer. We lived about five miles from the school and in the evenings I would walk home for the benefit of the exercise since I'd had to stop running. Phyllis helped me in countless ways; I stayed with her until I met back up with my sister, Pam. About a month before my due date I moved in with Pam and her husband, where I had my own room and contributed to my share of the rent. I was still having issues with my husband not calling although he would occasionally write.

My beautiful daughter was born on September 16 by cesarean, due to complications during delivery. In the absence of my husband, who wasn't able to return home until almost five weeks after she was born, Pam and Phyllis remained by my side through a night of difficult labor. I could not believe I was about to be a mother to this little alien that had been growing inside of me. But the drama didn't end with her birth: thanks to complications, I contracted a staph infection the day before my scheduled release. When I blacked out in the bathroom, the medical team went into action and determined I needed surgery. All of my vitals had dropped precipitously and I was clinging to life. Many people who cared about me converged on the hospital, including the pastor of my church who prayed over my bedside. My dear grandmother and countless others came to see me but I don't remember any of them being there. I was an awfully sick young lady though it wasn't until much later, when I was well out of the woods, that I realized how close I'd been to death.

In spite of my wonderful medical care, being in the hospital longer than expected was problematic because I did not have anyone to care for my baby daughter. Once again, my charming, handsome husband was MIA. The baby and I wound up staying at the hospital for 18 days but on different floors, which depressed and upset me. But after my blackout, they'd had no choice but to move me to another area and prevent me from seeing her until we were both released. Thankfully, my nurses were wonderful; they would give me little notes written as if they were from my daughter. Sometimes they would include her picture or an impression of her little footprints and they never failed to update me on her condition every day.

On the day of my release, Uncle Bernard, and Uncle Harold picked me up from the hospital. When we arrived at my building, they would not let me walk up to the third floor; one carried me while the other carried the baby and our belongings. Weeks later, I finally got word from my husband that he was coming home to see our newborn. It was a great reunion and I loved being with him. Again, he told me he was still trying to get me over to Germany. In preparation, I left my National Guard unit and transferred to the Inactive Reserve where I remained until sometime in 1984. After transferring to the IRR (Individual Ready Reserve), my husband informed me I would not be able to join him in Germany after all. Instead, he wanted me to go to Florida to be with his family until he returned. I was devastated and hurt: this latest development left me feeling unworthy of him and reinforced my fears that he was focused on anything but his wife and child.

A Sunshine State of Mind? Adjusting to Life in Saint Petersburg.

When I went to Florida to be closer to my then in-laws, my mother-in-law always bragged about me. She'd say, "This is my son's wife; isn't she pretty?" She was a beautician who had an incredible talent for doing hair; she also liked to dress stylishly. In her own way, she helped me go a little further in coming out of my shell.

My mother-in-law was the one who got me to go to the local education center to complete the work necessary to earn my high school diploma. She helped me find a job and got me involved in church. Did I ever need that sense of belonging! I needed to know what it was like to be close to a mother figure as an adult, especially since I was a new mother to a baby girl. Having that first child taught me more about unconditional love than any other experience I'd had. She loved and needed me in ways no other person did and she became my sole reason for surviving in – or more importantly – for conquering the world. She was mine and I was hers. She became my entire universe. To this point, my ex was absent in the sense that he was on tour in Germany. He did not call or write much. I know he said he loved me but his way of showing it was less than desirable. Our estranged relationship took its toll on me personally. Whether he realized it or not he reinforced insecurities, created trust issues, and brought out anger that created an unhealthy environment for our child and me. While I had moved forward significantly, self-esteem is a fragile thing; when you've struggled in that area of life, it is easy to slip backwards or experience a setback.

Upon arriving in the Sunshine State, I went through an adjustment period. The calmer, more sedentary lifestyle of Saint Petersburg presented a stark contrast to the one with which I was accustomed since birth. Still, I enjoyed meeting all of John's family and developed a close relationship with several of his sisters and his aunt. While some of us didn't always get along, my in-laws meant well. For a short while, I shared a place with one of John's sisters. When that didn't work out, I found a place to rent in preparation for his arrival later in the year. Since January of that same year, my husband had been sending home about six-hundred dollars per month – a huge help, but not enough to meet all of our needs.

As a private first class, he did not make enough money; therefore, working was a necessity for me. I first found employment at a department store before securing a full-time position with an insurance/title company. The plan was for John to get a job at the post office when he came home. For the first few weeks, it was great to have him back even though he seemed to have a hard time adjusting. All he wanted to do was take it easy which meant I had to put in longer hours to make ends meet. We couldn't afford the two-bedroom house or the furniture we'd been renting without his financial contributions. So we downgraded to a tiny, one-bedroom apartment. I can't remember how much it cost but moving there meant living in a seedy part of town.

As I said, John was having trouble transitioning back into civilian life. Little did I know, his constant drug use and excessive drinking would alter his demeanor and the way he interacted with me over time. For most of the first month, he didn't have a job and then he started preparing for the testing required by the postal service. Since he was a veteran, he was hired to be a mail sorter but still had to complete all of the training and testing. When he didn't last long, he blamed it on the fact that the work was just too stressful, but what I recently found out was that he failed the drug test. While I didn't know it then, it wouldn't have surprised me.

He loved hanging out with his friends. Many days I'd arrive home from work to find he was not there but down the street with them, drinking and smoking. To me, it seemed as if that was all they did most days even though that may not have been the case. However, I'd discover that my husband wasn't just spending time with the guys when I went looking for him one day. As I entered the building, his buddies eyed me strangely and when I inquired as to his whereabouts, no one wanted to give me a straight answer.

Finally, he emerged from one of the rooms with a woman. While I cannot state for certain what had transpired between them, it sure didn't make me feel warm and fuzzy. Whatever it was, it was nothing good: I left him there and took my child home. That night I slept with a knife under my pillow in anticipation of his potentially dangerous, drug-induced mental state when he returned to our apartment. I am not even sure he understood the fear I experienced when he was not in control; all I knew was that this wasn't the way I wanted to live, nor was it what I wanted for my child, who at the time shared a room with us. There were times when he'd get too rough but was too high to realize it. Thankfully, that night he heeded my warning to not touch me and went to sleep.

Our marriage was characterized by arguments about money, his behavior, and our life together. I hated it when John came home high because he was a different person – far from the charming, handsome man I'd fallen in love with. His sexual aggression terrified me because it brought back memories of the horror I'd endured at the hands of my brother. Would it have made a difference in the way he'd treated me if I'd told him about the rape? I can't say for sure. Fed up, I went back home with my parents the first time I left him. After being in Maryland for only two weeks, he persuaded me to return to Florida and my mother even convinced me it would be in my best interest to return. He promised he would change and told me he got a job. He swore we could make a fresh start and that he truly loved me.

Upon my return, I got a job at one of the factories assembling electronics circuit boards. One thing I was adept at was electronics and the use of testing equipment and soldering irons, which I learned from my classes in high school. My pay enabled us to live mostly on what I was making but things were still tough; sometimes I would have to borrow money from my mother-in-law to pay for diapers or milk. While we should have been on food stamps and assistance, that was unfamiliar territory for me; something my pride would not allow as long as I was able-bodied enough to work. While I'd been in Maryland, he'd moved to an upstairs apartment that was located in a bad area but right near the church I attended.

Well, the reunion was great but short-lived. Our arguments resumed when he went back to his old tricks. After a productive day at work, I'd come home to find folks hanging out in our apartment while our daughter would often be in the same clothes she'd been wearing when I left. Other times she was dirty. Obviously, whatever John was doing while I was at work often distracted him from taking care of our baby.

When the arguments turned into physical encounters, I knew it was time for me to leave for good. One night, we got into a huge fight that culminated with him putting his hands on me. I left and went to my sister-in-law's. Undeterred, he came looking for me and when he arrived at her place I was holding my daughter in my arms while drinking a beer to calm my nerves. I swear to this day he must've been on something pretty powerful because he would not let us go. He even tried to grab my baby out of my arms while he yelled at me, prompting his sister to step in between us and attempt to break his hold on our daughter. I handed the baby over to my sister-in-law, who safely got her away from him, and dealt with the situation as it was unfolding.

We got into another physical altercation and I told him it would be the last time this would happen. Then I warned him not to come home or I would call the police before taking my daughter and leaving for my home state. That evening I called my coworker to ask if I could stay with her until I could save the money for a plane ticket out of Florida. I packed some of our belongings, as many as I could, and left the next morning with no intention of going back. I did not want any further communication with him and I did not want him trying to persuade me to stay. Most importantly, I did not want another violent incident to occur. As soon as I received my next paycheck I bought a plane ticket to Washington DC. I left with my most precious possession, my daughter, with just one-hundred and ten dollars in my pocket. I had no idea where I was going to stay once I arrived but knew it would be the last time I lived in Saint Petersburg.

Developing and holding firm to an unshakeable belief in your self-worth after years of clinging to a deeply held feeling of total unworthiness is a monumental effort. You may think you have it totally under control, yet that little monster of self-doubt will rear its ugly head at the most inconvenient times. For me, it would always show up in my relationships with men: they would start out great but eventually, the guy would violate my trust on some level. Whether it was fooling around on me, lying to me, or treating me poorly, these incidents further eroded my self-esteem. I have battled with loving myself, and of thinking of myself as worthy and deserving for decades. And still to this day, the persistent little monster tries to hijack my feelings by filling my head with a multitude of insecurities. These self-esteem issues almost caused my current husband and me to split. I have always wondered what this extraordinary, handsome man is doing with someone like me and had never considered myself worthy of having someone like him.

After a specific incident resulted in the near destruction of our marriage, I knew I needed to address the foundational issue: me. In a case of perfect timing, it just so happened I was going on the first deployment to Kosovo and felt that the temporary separation would do us both a world of good. My husband had no idea how fragile my self-esteem was at this point, nor did he understand that his actions were critical for me to believe in us and our marriage.

He was unaware of my challenges in simply getting through each day. I cried going to work, at work, and coming home. I did not know how to put the monster back in the dungeon; thus, my internal battles raged until I left for the deployment. I was coping with my dislike of my body, self-doubt, and trust issues all over again – or maybe I never resolved them in the first place. I knew I had to deal with this in a way that would lead me to a better, healthier state of being; I also knew that no one else could do that but me. While deployments are tough, you learn something about yourself through the experience. For me, the deployment helped me to see myself through the eyes of others and draw upon the inner self-confidence that had ebbed and flowed in the past year. When I wasn't engaged in work, I could focus on the whole me – my physical, mental, and spiritual wellbeing – by exercising body, mind, and soul. This practice was crucial in order to return to my family as a more balanced woman than when I left.

I worked out most every day except Sunday, doing all types of different routines, gradually increasing my time from one hour to 90 minutes, and finally, two hours. On Sundays, I enjoyed a massage at the gym. While I did not attend religious service, I read my daily walks bible that I ordered after arriving – part of my effort to care for my spiritual wellbeing in addition to my mental and physical health. If an interviewer were to pose the question of what one specific habit got me through deployment, I would answer with my practice of faith. One day while watching Oprah, I heard her talking about a book called *The Secret* by Rhonda Byrne. Intrigued, I ordered it immediately and as soon as I read it, began practicing its recommendations.

I was also in the distance education program for the Army War College, which demanded a significant amount of my time with its assignments. When not studying, I filled the rest of my time by reading. After finishing *The Secret*, I started envisioning what I wanted for myself through meditation. I wrote notes to myself and posted them where I had to see them every day as reminders of my many goals: completing War College, building our dream home, becoming a general officer, earning a Ph.D., learning to swim, getting to a place where I was comfortable with just being me, and writing this book. This exercise required more than just creating a list; you had to create an action plan. For many of the items, developing an action plan was the easiest part. The mental aspects were much more difficult: I had to release my self-defeating beliefs, which meant I had to face the monster within. Confronting an enemy that had taken up residence in my head demanded more courage than dealing with deployment. It required me to let go of negative thoughts and emotions that had become ingrained in my everyday life. I can state with conviction that by the time I returned from the first deployment I was refocused, recommitted and confident in my own skin. It took a tremendous amount of effort to arrive at my goal but even now I am fully aware that it only requires one little setback to crack open the door for the monster once again.

CHAPTER 5

SEXUAL ASSAULT, RECOVERY, AND HEALING: MOVING BEYOND ABUSE

I was sixteen years old when it happened. Remember how I mentioned that my sister and I ran away from home several times to escape? What I didn't know then was that my wish would eventually be granted in the most horrific way possible.

While living under my parents' roof, one of my brothers used to stay with us during his military leave, a guy I used to think was the epitome of cool. During one fateful visit, I expressed my desire to go to my uncle's party and asked if he would take me since he had a car. When he agreed to my request, I was thrilled because although I had my license, I did not have access to transportation. Had he not been willing to drive me there, I would never have been able to go. On the ride over in his car we talked about how we never really had the chance to get to know each other because we grew up in separate households. There was nothing remotely unsettling about our conversation, nor did anything about the way we interacted at the party give me any indication of what would happen later that night.

But on the way home, I got a hint that something had changed when he began speaking to me differently. His flirtatiousness was both inappropriate and unanticipated, but I didn't know what to make of it. By the time we got home all I wanted to do was head for the safety of my bedroom, which I did as soon as we arrived. I closed the door behind me and got ready for bed. My mother had many strange rules, among them the dictate that we could only close our bedroom doors while changing; the rest of the time we had to leave them open, even while sleeping. This was one night I wish I would have disobeyed; then again, as I look back at the experience as an adult, I realize it was a painful but necessary occurrence on my path to leadership.

As far as I can remember, my brother was sleeping on the couch when I reluctantly left my door open and climbed under the covers. Not long after, he crawled into my bed. At first, I thought I was dreaming or imagining things because I'd been drinking at the party. But when he ordered me to be quiet and settled his body on top of mine, the realization of what was about to transpire filled me with panic, although I was too scared to yell or even utter a word. Anytime I indicated I might make a sound, he shushed me and told me, "Since we didn't grow up together I don't feel like we're related so it is OK."

Then he moved my pajama pants and underwear, placing his hands between my legs and in my vagina while he promised he would not hurt me. Yet he wouldn't *stop* hurting me. I heard him mumble empty compliments like, "You are so pretty," and "I am in love with you," before he parted my legs and entered me against my will. It didn't take him long to climax and climb off of me, but not before warning me to keep quiet about what he'd done because no one would believe me. I spent the rest of the night crying into my pillow.

The next day I completely avoided him, along with everyone else. I kept replaying the event over and over in my mind, berating myself for not knowing what to do. Consumed with fear and guilt, I believed it was my fault because I should have screamed, resisted, fought him, or simply done anything to make him stop. After he had left a few days later, I managed to get the courage up to tell my mother. I'd waited until I thought she was in a good mood, at least as good a mood as possible given her personality. She was not the type of mother in whom a daughter could confide her most intimate fears and secrets. Understanding the depth of her affection for him and the possibility that the rape could have impregnated me made it even more difficult but I also knew I didn't want him to come back ever again. Therefore, I told my mother everything.

At first, she was angry at my brother after I gave her my rundown of who, what, where, when, and how. I felt relieved that she would protect me by forbidding him to ever set foot inside our house again. In obedience to her order, I told my dad what had happened. He also believed me and expressed outrage. For a while at least, I thought my parents had my back.

But later that day as I was standing in the kitchen preparing fried chicken for dinner, I overheard my mother and father talking in the adjoining living room. I could tell she had been drinking. She began calling me terrible names like "slut" and "whore," suggesting that I had seduced him. "You probably wanted it to happen," she accused me. She demanded to know why I'd waited until after he left, which in her mind was proof of my guilt. If that wasn't bad enough, she followed that up with, "You're probably sleeping with your father."

Infuriated, my dad warned her, "You need to shut your mouth," which initiated a bitter fight between them. In the next moment, my mother picked up a huge glass ashtray and slammed it into his face. He then pushed her away and yelled at her to settle down but that only caused her to go after me with even more ferocity. Her repeated vicious accusations of being a whore and sleeping with my own father pushed me farther and farther to the edge until I finally lost it.

Hurt, shocked and mostly angry, I yelled back at her in defense of myself, which she perceived as an indication that I was about to come after her physically. She got up off of the couch and lunged toward me, prompting my father to step in between us before things did spiral out of control. At that moment, I was consumed with enough emotion to start throwing punches at my own mother; up to that point, I'd never thought of hitting her no matter how badly she treated me. But her vile insults, coupled with my trauma over being raped by a man I'd loved and trusted caused me to lose self-control. I thought of my sister, who by now had been placed in a foster home.

"I will kill you, I will kill you! Don't you even try to hold me back!" she screamed at my father.

My dad looked at me and stated plainly, "You need to leave. You need to leave now."

With that, I grabbed my coat and walked out the door. I had no time to gather any of my belongings; I literally left that house with the clothes on my back. I don't remember much else about that night other than the fact it had been one more occasion during which my parents fought with each other and I was to blame. It ultimately set off a chain reaction of events that would alter the course of my life and unleashed memories I'd either suppressed or had just flat-out forgotten.

Good Touch, Bad Touch: Come Take a Walk with Me

To the best of my memory, I was about five or six years old when it first happened, back when I lived with my grandparents in the woods on about 26 acres. It might have happened sooner than I can recall; perhaps I was just too young to remember anything prior. Up until now, I've shared only idyllic stories of my rural, poor childhood but for many years, I'd repressed some not-so-good memories too.

Like I said, my uncles were my entire world at that time and the only thing I wanted to do was make them happy. To me, everything started and stopped with them. I admired and loved them. Whenever they asked me to do something, I wouldn't hesitate because I trusted them. Being on the receiving end of their attention filled me with joy as a child. One of our favorite activities was walking in the woods. I loved these outings...but not when other things happened.

I recall being out in the woods with one of my uncles when he'd tell me to take my pants down. He would then expose himself and pull me onto his lap. My only memories involve him sliding against my vagina but never penetrating me. He would do this until he ejaculated; then he'd clean me up and tell me I was a "good girl."

At that age all I craved was praise and approval; I didn't understand whether or not this was right or wrong. I trusted him. These incidents took place numerous times but I don't remember when they actually started or stopped.

Sit in My Lap

As I already mentioned, many of my uncles lived at home and I loved them all dearly. Creating more opportunity for inappropriate behavior and sexual abuse of a child was the fact that we only had three sleeping rooms in the house: one for my grandparents and two for the rest of us. While only a few of my uncles took advantage of me, when these repressed memories came flooding back, I realized that was enough.

Aside from the walks in the woods, I remember another almost identical encounter which I'm fairly certain took place when I was around seven years old though I cannot recall the number of times. I used to play house, hide and seek, Cowboys and Indians, or with my paper dolls. One day in particular, I was upstairs playing with my paper dolls when another uncle came into the room where we all slept. It was just the two of us, alone together. He asked me what I was doing and told me to come and sit in his lap.

I did as I was told because he indicated that he would tell if I didn't obey. He then pulled me into his lap, holding me tight while he grinded himself against my buttocks with just enough force to satisfy himself. The entire time he'd warn me to be quiet, presumably so he could listen for someone coming up the steps as I now understand in hindsight. Once he finished, he would tell me to go downstairs.

While the above incidents would most likely outrage decent people, as a child, I didn't see them as sexual abuse. I loved my uncles and wanted to be just like them. Now as a grown woman, I have reached an understanding that abuse manifests itself in a variety of ways and often disguises itself in such a manner that the victim doesn't even realize they've been violated. Looking back, I wonder if as a child I internalized my discomfort with these occurrences. Could they have been the underlying cause of my bedwetting issues?

As I've mentioned previously, while living with my grandparents, no one ever berated me for wetting the bed. But as with everything else, once I was taken away from their home and forced to live with my mother everything changed. Whereas my grandmother would comfort and assure me it was all okay when I wet the bed, my mother would yell at me for being "too lazy to get up at night" and blame my grandparents for the problem. To further rub salt into my wound, she'd then hang the urine-stained sheets out the window. Imagine the horror I felt as a nine-year-old girl, seeing the delight my mother would take in embarrassing me. While I believe I stopped wetting the bed around the age of ten, I never forgot her reaction in the aftermath of every incident – just one more dramatic contrast between my mother and grandmother.

You are Just Like "Them"

Webster's Dictionary defines verbal abuse as "language that condemns or vilifies usually unjustly, intemperately, and angrily."

Abuse takes many forms: degrading, belittling, name-calling, loud rants for the purpose of silencing into submission; and from obvious put-downs to not-so-obvious remarks that dehumanize the person to whom it is directed.

Once taken out of my grandparents' environment and into my parents' home I was exposed to my mother's extremely temperamental behavior. From the sixth to tenth grades, a critical juncture in every child's life, I had to cope with verbal abuse and the belief that my mother really didn't like me. Therefore, my punishment was being forced to live with her.

I didn't know how to deal with the irrational rants and behaviors, which were at times focused on me and other times on someone or something else. When directed at me they started out in the forms of insults like, "You are just like them." Them, as I've stated, referred to my father's family whom my mother regarded as beneath her.

From there it became, "You ole yellow girl," "You act like a boy," "You are ignorant," "You're stupid just like them," and "You are no good." The worst part of all was that I never figured out what triggered the behavior, which instilled fear in me of saying anything. I did not necessarily talk unless spoken to and sometimes I'd whisper my feelings to my siblings only to have her chide me, "I hear you talking to them," "You can't talk," "Why are you always poking out your mouth?"

These verbally abusive encounters escalated to the point where my youngest brother would mimic her behavior. He'd call me the same names and make fun of me. It was incredibly hurtful and resulted in my learning how to be an intensely angry person during the early years of my transition from living with my grandparents to living with my parents and siblings.

Although my mother never beat me, there were times when she would push a fist into my face to make her point; once in a while, she'd slap me because of the way I'd look at her. She failed to understand how much I feared her and that I didn't want to do anything that drew attention to me for any reason.

At night when I went to bed, I would sometimes pray for God to take me out of this awful place. There were times when I would cry silently because I missed the solace my grandparents provided. Running away with my sister seemed like the right answer because, in my mind, my mother did not want me.

Lessons Learned

Abuse is abuse, whether verbal, sexual, or physical. Verbal abuse can be much more subtle yet far more damaging in the longer term. Out of fear of disappointment and being a "bad girl," I never told anyone about these encounters until now. I have since learned that you must find and confide in someone you trust; you must tell them what is happening or has already happened. You are worthy and you have every right to stand up for yourself. You can say "no."

Today, I am my own person: unique, loveable, and respected. I have come to realize abuse in any form is *never* okay. Incest is incest and is always wrong; it doesn't matter whether you grew up together or not.

As a parent, I've learned the importance of teaching your children the difference between good touch and bad touch at an early age and I've tried to impart these lessons to them. Hurtful words have the power to impact your self-esteem and confidence until you feel as if you aren't worth the dirt beneath your feet. Parents, it is never acceptable to degrade, ridicule, or call your children names. Your job is to protect and support them, not bully them into submission.

Enough is Enough

I fully understood and applied the meaning of the phrase, "The buck stops with me" when my youngest brother came to live with me after he graduated from high school. Part of our deal was for him to obtain the technical training he needed to get a good job and provide for himself and to watch my daughter when I had to work evenings. I bought him an old car to drive and paid for his program at Lincoln Tech, determined to help him get a good foundation. He'd had learning challenges his entire life and I wanted to do whatever I could to help.

During the early stages of his stay with me, he did make a go of it. Unfortunately, somewhere along the line, he started doing drugs. While I didn't know exactly what he was using, I informed him if he kept it up he would have to leave my home. When summer rolled around, I headed out for my two weeks of training with the Army Reserves and left my daughter in the care of my sister. When we had the opportunity to speak by phone, she told me she had something bad to tell me which caused my heart to immediately skip a beat. I wasn't sure what had happened but I had a sinking feeling it would be gut-wrenching.

I listened as she proceeded to tell me she'd caught my daughter touching herself, which she felt was abnormal behavior given her young age. When she asked where she had seen that, my daughter replied that her uncle would often touch her there. As I listened, I felt the rage and anger welling up inside; I knew that if I got a hold of him, I would kill him. Prior to informing me about this distressing news, my sister had confided in my mother; both of them agreed that if I somehow found him before the police, it would be all over.

When I returned a few days later, I sat my daughter down so I could hear for myself her version of events before I contacted the police to file a report and press charges. They picked him up and the county sent personnel to our home to obtain information on what had happened. Although they found no damage to her private area during a medical examination, they told me that the level of detail she had provided proved it was impossible for her to have made it up. Thus, we agreed to move forward and began preparations for a trial.

But unknown to me, an unexpected development would foil our plans.

One evening the case worker paid a visit to our home to announce that she had something for me to read. It was a letter written by my mother essentially discrediting me as an individual and a mom. Yes, in her own written words she described me as an unfit parent, a "slut" and a "whore" who was taking drugs and unworthy of raising a child. She recommended that child services take her away from me.

The case worker explained that even though her letter was filled with lies, we'd have an uphill battle ahead of us with my mother supporting him. On her recommendation, we made the decision to get him on the list as a potential sex offender so that if he were ever picked up again on a similar charge he would then be registered as a sex offender. Although I felt as if justice wasn't being served for my daughter, the thought of putting her through the turmoil of taking the stand and describing what he'd done to her to a bunch of strangers was simply too much. Based on my own experience, I didn't have the heart to put her in that position.

In the end, justice was served because he committed the same offense against someone else's child...and this time, his luck ran out. He has since spent time in jail for numerous charges including sexual abuse.

When I first became aware of his crimes, I immediately knew

"the buck stopped with me." It was time to end the cycle of abuse once and for all. Having done everything within my power to help my brother, I learned a hard lesson: you cannot want more for another human being than they want for themselves. But more importantly, I realized I had to be the one to put a stop to this deviant behavior, no matter how difficult. When I struck that deal with my brother I had no idea that he would do such a thing, even given our family history. But unlike my mother, I wasn't willing to defend the indefensible. Thankfully today, my daughter is thriving.

Sexual Harassment in the Workplace

While sexual harassment in the workplace is the focus of much attention these days, there was a time when it was mostly swept under the carpet. Years ago, in one of my places of employment I worked as a program analyst in radar and sonar systems installation for a defense contractor supporting a naval program. I reported directly to the manager with whom I also collaborated on these projects. Due to the nature of our work, we were required to travel from time to time.

My client was great to work with until he started to exhibit strange behavior. Likely due to my upbringing, I have always been an early bird. In this job, I'd invariably arrive at the office before 7 a.m. and in many cases, I was the first person to show up. I fell into a routine of either heading to my client's office or having him meet me at mine in the morning. Eventually, it got to the point where on a daily basis he would want to go to lunch with me or bring his lunch to eat at my desk while I worked. Then I noticed he began arriving at work earlier and spending most of his time in my workspace. Although annoyed by his constant presence, I didn't want to piss off the client and simply dealt with it.

However, I was completely unprepared when he decided to take things to a whole new level. It happened during a business trip that consisted of several stops, with a final destination of San Diego. After being on the road with him for almost a week, it was impossible to escape; one evening over dinner in San Diego he started to make inappropriate advances like attempting to hold my hand and walking too close for comfort. I kept thinking, "Please just let me get away from him because we head home tomorrow."

Back at the hotel, he walked me to my room since it was right next to his. Just as I turned to open the door, he tried to kiss me. I pushed him away immediately and said, "No, don't. You're a nice guy but you are my client." Thankfully he didn't press the situation but he did give me the cold shoulder the next day.

When I got back to my office, I told my supervisor what had happened. Unfortunately, instead of supporting me, he advised me not to make a big deal out of it because he was our client. I requested a reassignment but he denied it, informing me that I must continue to support the client in spite of what he'd done. Eventually, I did get reassigned to another team and client but I never received any support from my superiors to file a formal complaint.

Emerging Leadership

As a new commander of the maintenance company, I was deeply involved in ensuring that my soldiers were engaging in the required activities to help them meet challenges such as height and weight mandates and physical training. In this capacity, my first sergeant and I discussed action plans for each individual with their section leads. I took over command at times when our absences were high and drill attendance was not where it should be. Focusing in on the problem areas such as personnel standards was a key leader responsibility. I did not treat any of my soldiers differently than others and when someone needed assistance, I ensured that they had the necessary resources. If it meant I had to go pick them up for drill, then that is exactly what I did.

However, it seems that not everyone took my results-oriented methods in the right way. I remember one specialist who seemed to think he could say and do whatever he wanted since I was a female, regardless of the fact that I was his commander. In the beginning, the incidents occurred infrequently. The first took place while we were conducting unit weigh-in. I was in the room with only a few personnel, mainly my problem children, to ensure that they were weighing in. I knew exactly who could pass weight and who needed to be tape-tested for body-fat compliance. When it was this specialist's turn, I advised the tester that he did not need to be taped – to which the specialist unnecessarily replied loudly enough for many of the guys around him to hear, "I have something for you to tape."

Before I could even say anything, one of the noncommissioned officers told me he would take care of it and pulled him out of the room. For this instance, they counseled him on his disrespectful behavior. Apparently he was not deterred because during another drill he left flowers on my chair in my office area. Worse, they weren't just any flowers but flowers pulled from the bed right outside our building. The first sergeant and I had a conversation with the specialist's supervisor and told them that he was not to come anywhere near my office or I would be moving forward with disciplinary action. Things calmed down for months, then right after our December holiday meal, my daughters and I sat in our car amid a long line waiting to head out. Brazenly, he walked up to my open window on my side of the car to wish me happy holidays, followed by an attempt to reach into the window and grab me as if to kiss me. I immediately warned him that if he didn't move, I was going to put the window up on his neck. Before waiting for his reply, I pushed the power button up and drove off. The soldier was counseled again.

For a while, everything settled down and there were no more instances until our annual training the following summer. During annual training, we conducted health and welfare inspections. When his area was inspected, we found empty beer cans and liquor bottles in his wall locker; in violation of our policy, he had obviously been drinking. In my mind, this was the last straw. After annual training, I reviewed all of the disciplinary items that needed to be closed out. We were working on his disciplinary action for violating general orders during annual training.

Early one morning I received a phone call at my civilian job from this specialist and it was obvious that he had already been drinking. When I asked him how he got my work number, he just ignored my question and began ranting about how much he loved me and wished I would give him a chance. After reading him the riot act, I hung up the phone.

Before I could even gain my composure, he called again and I completely I lost it. This time, he raved on about wanting to suck my toes, lick my lips, and many other things that are just too embarrassing to even think or write about. I yelled at him at the top of my lungs that he was never to call me again – an exchange heard by my whole office. I then called our legal team at our higher headquarters and told them what had happened. The judge advocate I spoke with tried to convince me not to move forward with disciplinary action because this soldier had 18 years of service. I replied that I didn't care and warned him that if he did not prepare the paperwork, he would also be subjected to disciplinary action. I reminded him that this guy had gone beyond harassment; at this point, he was borderline stalking me. Who knew what he would do next?

In an interesting twist, that same day the specialist himself called the state headquarters to talk to legal and admitted that he thought he made a pass at his commander.

YOU THINK!!

After all was said and done, he ended up with numerous Article 15's and was discharged out of the guard.

We Are Survivors

Sometimes no matter how hard you try to prevent bad things from happening, they just do. In my life, I struggled to understand why I had to deal repeatedly with all kinds of abuse, from verbal to physical to sexual.

Why me, dear God? Why are you not protecting me?

Soon I started to believe I deserved it and fell into victimhood mode rather quickly. When my life took a positive turn in the years following these abusive incidents, it enabled me to lock the painful memories of the past in a remote area of my subconscious mind, presumably for good. It was not until recent years that I started to deal with them in a meaningful way, in part by using my experiences as a teaching point for others. I wanted abuse survivors to understand that rape, incest, molestation and other sexual crimes can happen to anyone. While I frequently talk about these situations, I have stopped referring to myself as the victim. In fact, others have helped me change my terminology from being the victim to being a survivor.

Yes, I am a survivor of sexual abuse. Making the decision to refuse to tolerate this type of behavior does not make me the villain. Actually, it makes me the hero because I have the fortitude and the courage to stand up to my abusers. I no longer feel ashamed, they are no longer in control, and when they see me, they have to look me in the eyes while pretending that it did not happen. They have to live with the fact that I know what they did was wrong. This is no longer a burden on my subconscious; in fact, I have found that you can gain immense strength from overcoming. I am a survivor. We are all survivors.

CHAPTER 6

FINDING ME – THE LONG JOURNEY HOME

It took many years to arrive at a point where I genuinely started to come into my own. Initially, as a single mother with a toddler and no place to call home, I dealt with tremendously difficult obstacles. Since I didn't have a car, I wanted to stay in DC to take advantage of the transit system, which would make it easier for me to get around. After several weeks in the area, I still didn't have a place to live or a job. As a temporary measure, I stayed with my sister for several nights in her room on Fort Meyer. I didn't want to get her in trouble, but I also didn't want to be on the street. In an effort to be helpful, she recommended that I stay with my brother who lived in the city, unaware that he was the same person who had sexually abused me years prior. From what I can recall, she and I had never discussed the incident.

With no other viable options and a strong desire to get my daughter and me off of the streets, I agreed to move into his one-room efficiency with a shared bathroom down the hall. He assured me we could stay there as long as necessary. Although we had to sleep on the floor, it was better than the alternative. I found a job through a temp agency working at the gas company in DC and put my daughter into daycare. Unfortunately, I soon discovered that once I paid for child care, bus transportation, and food, there was nothing left. At the time, I was making about $120 - $140 a week. Sometimes I would walk the ten blocks to the daycare center just to save money.

My oldest sister wanted to help me out and agreed to take care of my daughter until I could get a better job and a place to live. Her generosity, however, did not last long. You see, up to this point she only had two boys and wanted a girl. So she made me an offer she thought I couldn't refuse given my dire circumstances: sign over custody of my baby to her so she could raise her as her daughter. While I love my sis dearly, this was a bridge too far. After some time, she informed me that if I could not pay her something in return for my daughter staying there, then I would have to take her back. She announced that she was bringing her back to my brother's place where I was living. I was at a loss because I knew this was not the best thing for my child; I also knew that the emotional turmoil I was going through was not good for me either. He would constantly tell me I was cramping his style with the women and that I needed to make up for it. As much as I dreaded being on the street in the wintertime with my daughter, I knew I had to get out because tensions were escalating; I was terrified of what might happen. I am not sure how long I stayed with him or even how long this whole situation played out.

One day I met a guy who worked at the gas company. Like many of the meter readers, he would talk to me almost every day because of the department I worked in. During a conversation on one particular occasion, I told him I was looking for a cheap place to rent and he replied that he might know someone who could help me – one of the other guys who was into real estate and had several rentals. I ended up renting the basement from him with use of his kitchen. It was a good deal but the only problem was that this place was on the outskirts of DC, just into Maryland. Things were going OK but getting through the daily grind of life was rather tedious: I had to take several buses to get to the babysitter and then to work. Eventually, it took a financial toll because while the funds were better, they were still not great. When I realized the money I was making was not enough to take care of her, I did the thing I dreaded most – I called my husband and asked him for help.

He asked if he could fly up to talk with me and I agreed. During his visit, we mutually decided that he would take care of our daughter until I got a stable place. After he had taken her back to Florida, I cried for days. I felt like a horrible mother for letting her go but I could not, *would not* see her on the streets with me if that was where I was going to end up. This job was only temporary and I didn't know what was going to happen when the lady I was filling in for came back from maternity leave. I had to have the peace of mind of knowing my daughter was taken care of while I focused on getting myself into a better position. I did not want her to live like this and found some small measure of comfort knowing she was at least with family who loved her and would help her father tend to her needs. But this was only for a short while; I could do anything for a short while.

When my assignment at the gas company ended, the temp agency found me another assignment as a receptionist for a different company, a development I hadn't anticipated. Something else I hadn't planned on? The guy with whom I'd been talking on a regular basis at the gas company was going to ask me out on a date. Although he was seventeen years older than me, he was a complete gentleman. While we were an item, he helped me in significant ways: through his emotional support and encouragement and his demonstration of how a man should treat a woman – with respect and dignity. I doubt I could ever repay him for his kindness and generosity.

He even helped me get a car and celebrated with me when

my temp position became a permanent job offer. He taught me how to dress and sent me to modeling school which helped me to discover and appreciate my outside beauty. Having been through his own divorce, he supported me through the process of ending my marriage and securing full custody of my daughter. His sister became one of my best friends and my most trusted confidant. Under their friendship and mentoring, I began to flourish. I took courses at a business school to improve my chances of a better career. I got a promotion on my job from receptionist to learning contracts management, not realizing that this would form the foundation for a prominent career many years later. Unknown to me, this promotion would also change my perception of myself, at least externally. Yet while I had strong feelings for this man, I did not want to be in a steady relationship.

It was important to me to be on my own for a while. Additionally, I knew our relationship would not last over the long haul due to our age difference and the fact that he did not want to be tied down with a small child. We had different dreams: he wanted to settle into domesticity and I needed to live a little. When my daughter came to live with us, we just grew apart. Although he was crazy about her, the seventeen-year age differential was too much to overcome. In a testament to the solid friendship we'd built, it was an amicable split; he even helped me get an apartment in the same building. For years to come we remained good friends, with him riding to my rescue on several occasions – even accompanying me on multiple visits to my parents. By now, my relationship with my mother had improved but was still far from perfect.

Pathological Dysfunction Leads to an Inevitable Outcome

During this time, I received a dreadful call one evening. I don't remember exactly who phoned to tell me my father was in shock trauma in Baltimore, but they didn't think he was going to make it and advised me to get there as soon as possible. When I asked what had happened, they informed me that they didn't have the full story but my mother had been taken into custody. As it turns out, she shot him twice at close range with a shotgun. There were all kinds of emotions going through me: anger, fear, despair, and still more anger. I knew they had a tumultuous relationship but never thought it would end like this. I was not able to see my father until the next morning when he asked for me, which hurt my other sisters but I brushed it off and went in to see him. He began by giving me instructions to make arrangements to get my mother out. I told him I would do no such thing until he told me what happened. He said it was an accident and that he was not going to press charges.

I'm sorry but in my mind, something must've happened to drive her to this breaking point. There is much more to this story but I was only able to get bits and pieces, which only enraged me further. I told him I would visit her but would not be the one to get her out; if that's what he wanted, then he would have to recruit someone else. In the end, I did go to visit her and tried to get her to tell me the truth, with no success. She got mad at me for making accusations about what happened but I stood my ground and wouldn't budge. To me it was nothing but drama – and I refused to endure any more of my parents' dramatics now that I was a grown woman who didn't have to succumb to their pressure. I was my own person. While distancing myself from them again hurt deeply, I knew I had to do it. Our relationship went on a hiatus for some time after this incident. It was not until my brother graduated from school that we talked again.

Climbing the Corporate Ladder: Learning to Engage my Brain First, My Mouth Second

Because of the training I received and the experience I gleaned with contracts management, my career continued to blossom. Soon I got a new job in program and contracts management with better pay and good benefits, allowing me to become even more self-sufficient as a single parent. I truly began to learn what it was like to be valued and wanted as an employee. I discovered that I was good at dealing with clients and thoroughly enjoyed working in the acquisition area. During this time, I also started back as a drilling reservist. I continued to grow my career and was quickly promoted to specialist.

While it seemed my professional life was on the upswing, I jumped too quickly into another relationship that turned out to be too good to be true. Against my better judgment, I let him convince me to move in with him and his daughter. I should have known better than to give up my apartment I so very much wanted. But he convinced me that I'd be able to save money and that it would be a better place for my child. Well, I think all he wanted was a live-in babysitter because soon after we moved in, he started going out and leaving me with the kids, which included his son by another woman who would come for visits every other weekend. During one of those weekends when we had all of his kids and my daughter, he announced he was heading out. When I asked him where he was going, he wouldn't tell me, but later I found two concert tickets on his dresser for that evening. I asked him who he was taking to the concert and he told me it was none of my business. He tried to grab the tickets out of my hand, but I took them and announced, "If you think I am going to watch your kids again while you go out, you have another thing coming." Then I ripped them in half. He then slapped me and threw me toward the bed before taking the tickets and storming out.

I knew I'd made a big mistake and needed to make plans to get out of there ASAP. After I tried and failed to get back into my old apartment building due to a waiting list, I got an apartment in the Oxon Hill area with an immediate vacancy. I called a few of my friends to ask for their help with moving. The day they came to help me move out, my soon-to-be ex-boyfriend and I got into a huge argument. He'd been watching us like a hawk, observing every item we were taking out, including the video player I had brought. I wasn't about to leave any expensive items with him, even those that were gifts at the time. Angrily, he grabbed the video player and we started to struggle over it. He then pushed me and I hit him with enough force to cause him to grab his face, although he didn't let go. My friends pulled me away and got in between us before he called the police and ordered us to leave. He filed charges against me, resulting in a bench warrant for my arrest. I went to the jail when I received it and they released me. I also went to court but not before I filed a civil suit to get the rest of my belongings. When we showed up in court, I told the judge that he pushed me when we were fighting over the video player. I also explained what led up to the situation and what prompted me to hit him.

Of course, his story was completely different. He even got one of his friends to lie that I hit him first before he pushed me. After listening to both sides, the judge made us come to an agreement: I would drop the civil suit and he would drop the charges because this was clearly a domestic dispute that should never have gotten to this point. Let's just say I got lucky this time for many reasons. This little incident could have ended my military career if I had been charged. Regardless of whether he was pushing on me, my actions were not appropriate either. I was leaving because he put his hands on me but at that point in time, I provoked him by tearing up the tickets. Yes, he was stepping out on me but I realized that every action caused a reaction whether good or bad. This was another moment of choice: I decided from that point forward, I would not give any man a fair shot. I was going to treat them the way they'd been treating me. Additionally, I realized I had to stand on my own two feet and refuse to ever be dependent on any man ever again. However, it was also up to me to learn how to control my temper – or, at least, engage my brain before engaging my mouth. I also figured out I did not want a relationship with a man I could not trust, no matter how charming, handsome, or intelligent. In that sense, I didn't want to be like my parents, whose volatile relationship centered around co-dependency, abuse, denial, and enabling. Yet for some inexplicable reason, I seemed to be drawn to men who were essentially no good.

While I did not date again right away, I started working more and more based on some goals I had set for myself. Ultimately, I took in my younger brother after he graduated high school in an effort to help him get a good start in life. I took on part time jobs in security guard work, teaching aerobics, and even working at a furniture store on some weekends – basically anything I could possibly do to get ahead. When I dated, I was quick to ditch a guy if he had any kind of quirk or just seemed to be clueless. I was a frequent client at a club in Camp Springs Maryland called *Classics*. My favorite spot, I'd go there at least twice a week and met several folks I would hang out with. One of them was involved in local level politics and she got me involved in supporting a few folks running for county executive and delegates. I helped to organize a dinner and fashion show for the guy running for county executive. Along with a few others, I cooked all of the food for the event and I organized the fashion show. It was a wonderful, successful event, and while he didn't win the election, it was an enriching experience.

As a result of my interactions, I met an increasing number of accomplished people and started to realize that I *could* be more if I *wanted* to be more. I discovered I loved being amongst the professionals and wanted to figure out how I could become more like them. I also hung out with several of the players from the Washington Wizards. The best thing about these guys? They loved to have fun and would not get too involved. This was my time to enjoy being single, which worked out rather well until I met a wonderful guy – not your run-of-the-mill player – for whom I eventually fell head over heels. We met in the Classics night club, where I was hanging out in my usual spot, totally bored with the whole scene. That is until I just so happened to look over and spotted a guy who should have been any place but here. He had dreamy black hair down to his shoulders which immediately caught my attention. I tried to work up the courage to talk to him but was not even sure he spoke English.

Instead of being straightforward, I asked his friend to pass on a message to him. We met outside the club and immediately seemed to hit it off. We talked the whole night about where he was from and what he was doing. I was not used to this type of man, one who was gentlemanly and respectful. Most of the guys I would meet in the club were total duds and annoying, to say the least. But this one was incredibly intriguing. They say that you have to kiss your fair share of toads to get a prince. Well, this was one prince who didn't kiss me for almost four months – not even a peck on the cheek, nothing. With that said, I am sure you can wait to hear about us in more detail but for now, I'll admit that I had no idea that this man would play such a significant role in my life going forward.

Even though I continued to hang out at the club, I made a decision to go to college. I first started out at Southeastern University and then transferred to Columbia Union College, which is now Washington Adventist College. I also took a few courses at Charles Community College and University of Maryland University College to get the courses needed to complete my undergraduate degree. Southeastern required me to put together a portfolio in order for my prior school and work credits to be evaluated. They took all of my credits from the business school and some from work to apply them towards my degree. This was important because it gave me hope of actually getting my bachelors. At any given time, I was taking a full complement of classes. I started school in September of 1985 and completed my bachelors in December of 1994. It was a long, hard road. As I said, in many cases I was working multiple jobs along with the military to get this done – not to mention I also remarried and had another daughter during this timeframe. As a matter of fact, I was taking several classes while I was pregnant in hopes of getting through them before delivering.

Dual Careers, Endless Growth Opportunities

My civilian work was going well but I was getting somewhat antsy in my reserve unit. I gained an enormous amount of experience working in other units and numerous civilian jobs. The key thing I learned is that you don't make a job or role change without there being an opportunity to grow and learn from the experience. But getting to that was not as easy as it seemed. I worked in a variety of roles, starting as clerical support, office manager, junior engineer, program analyst, contracts manager, senior analyst, and systems analyst which all led up to being a senior consultant with a consulting firm. Most of my roles focused on program management, contracts management and negotiations, financial management and information systems design, development, and testing.

Many required me to work closely with clients on a daily basis. My clients ranged from the Department of Defense, local government, civilian government, and private industry. I considered every role I had as a stepping stone or building block for what was coming next. I grew and learned with each one I took on, starting with my receptionist position that led to a 14% raise to become the office manager. I also provided support to the engineering staff at the Naval Sea Systems Command. This was also my first foray into government contracting because we lost a major contract to a competitor. One of the engineers asked me to join him at the new company that won the contract so I made the change because they offered me a considerable amount more than what I was making.

At the new company, I provided acquisition, configuration

management, logistics and program planning for the same client but supporting the Surface Anti-Submarine Warfare Combat Systems Program Office. As was the case with defense contracting work, when contract options were not renewed or the contract was up for bid again, it would frequently go to another prime contractor. Therefore, I had another opportunity to move with several others to another company supporting the Cruise Missile Project within Naval Sea Systems Command. This contract ended in October of 1990, presenting a huge dilemma for me because of the timing and where I was at that time with my military career. I did not want to take on another job since I was going to graduate from officer candidate school less than seven months from that time and would then need to be gone for four months for school. So I decided to consult on my own and work for Spa Lady full-time as an assistant manager to give me the flexibility I needed to go to officer candidate school.

While I found I had a good rapport with clients, I was also a smart leader who wasn't afraid to take on new responsibilities. I was a quick study whose personality was tailored to being in the client service industry. The more I learned, the more I wanted to step out of my comfort zone and into the black galaxy. The experience I gained in the many years prior served as the foundation for a longstanding career with one of the largest global consulting firms in the business today.

As for my professional appearance, I'd have to admit that in the beginning my dress was subpar, mostly because I did not have the adequate cash flow to purchase nice business suits. I eventually found one store that had *three-for* specials on suits. I would layaway and pay for three outfits every quarter in order to improve my business wardrobe. I took courses and read professional books on how to dress in the office. I shopped with other professional women and emulated those who dressed the part. I became my own project and discovered that I enjoyed being and looking like a professional. While I worked on the outside, the inside me still needed much focus; I did not realize how much until various issues arose that required me to give a little more of myself.

While getting my civilian career off the ground, I rejoined the military in 1985 after being in the inactive reserve for a number of years. I joined the 2290th Army Hospital in Rockville. I had enrolled in that unit when I first came back to the DC area and then transferred to a closer unit because of transportation issues. The second unit was the 226th MI Detachment in Forestville Maryland. This was a much smaller unit where I performed admin support tasks in support of the security officer. I made the rank of specialist when I was at this company and started training in the counterintelligence field. In 1988, they sent me to Primary Leadership Training (PLDC) so I could get promoted to sergeant.

My leadership skills emerged and I completed PLDC in the top 5% of my class. But I did not get my promotion to sergeant. I decided it was time to get laser-focused if I was going to work in my field as a personnelist and transferred back to the 2290th after being gone for several years. There I had an enormous amount of support and would often be asked to work additional time supporting the operations and training section. I finally made the Sergeant's Board in 1989 with hopes of making sergeant.

As I mentioned, I received tremendous support and encouragement. There were several individuals whom I feel contributed to me making the decision to go to officer candidate school: my first sergeant and my section officer in charge. They convinced me I had good leadership skills and should seriously consider becoming an officer. Though skeptical, I decided to look into the program and found I would have to go away to officer candidate school, which would be an issue since I was a single parent. The second option that presented itself was going to the officer candidate school with the National Guard. Ultimately, I had a choice to make that would affect my military career for a long time to come.

I made the decision to make the leap before I found out the results of the Sergeant's Board. I transferred back to the Maryland National Guard in hopes of being selected to attend officer candidate school in the state. I joined the 629th MI Battalion in December of 1989. I was boarded for officer candidate school in January of 1990 and started pre-officer candidate school in February of 1990. This move automatically promoted me to staff sergeant for the whole time as an officer candidate. The actual school started in May of 1990 and we graduated on July 27, 1991. This was a significant and major milestone that transformed my military career. It was through this journey that I found the true leader in myself and I graduated in the top of the class. I walked away with distinguished graduate, outstanding graduate, and the leadership award. This was a huge accomplishment but it also meant that my daughter and I would be separated again while I attended school.

Three days after graduating, I left for ordnance officer basic course in Aberdeen, Maryland and my daughter headed to Florida to stay with her grandmother for the school year. While this was a tough decision, it was the right one. I knew her grandmother loved her and would take excellent care of her. She wanted to help me out and without her assistance, I would not have been able to go to my basic course. Prior to completing my basic course, I started applying for jobs with my newfound skills added to my resume. I highlighted my end-user experience with several logistics and maintenance systems. These newly added skills landed me a job working with a company that specifically focused on logistics or supply chain as we now know it. The program I was hired to support was working on the external interface team and ran the interfaces test lab for the Reserve Component Automation System (RCAS). This opportunity increased my knowledge, skills and abilities across both the military and civilian sector.

My next guard assignment enhanced my experience because I went to the 729th Forward Support Battalion in Hagerstown as a maintenance officer and stayed there until August of 1992 when I transferred to the 229th Main Support Battalion as the Maintenance Control Officer. I soon took over as the maintenance company executive officer. This was another key move because it was not long before I became the company commander of that organization as a first lieutenant with about two-and-a-half years' time in grade. My leadership career from this point forward was fairly fast. I ensured that all of my military and civilian education met or exceeded all requirements and mapped out the assignments that would be crucial to my ongoing professional progress. Additionally, I took on extra duties and tasks to stand out from my peers. These deliberate, purposeful choices got me noticed by leadership as being a good, solid leader. I also developed the reputation for being tough yet fair to my soldiers.

After working on RCAS for a little over two years, I was in the market for another job when I received the two promising job offers I mentioned earlier. That was when I began a more than 20-year career with one of the big five consulting firms. Without these experiences, I would not have been positioned to obtain the roles I did. Overall it was not as easy as it is described because I had to learn a significant amount of information in a very short period. But I will say that for the most part, I was well-prepared for the roles I took on. Some of them were definitely a stretch; it made me nervous to step out of my comfort zone but I soon found that in consulting, you very seldom worked in your comfort zone.

When I interviewed with the consulting firm, the extent of my experience was working with defense contractors. I had not experienced the consulting life and had no idea what to expect. At the time, I had received two job offers: one with a program and team I knew well in the same job I had been doing for several years; the other with the global consulting firm, doing work I was familiar with. It was a difficult choice because I wasn't sure what the differences in the two jobs would really be. A friend of mine convinced me to take the job with the consulting company which came with many challenges my first few years. I started with them as a senior consultant which meant that I was given credit for a certain amount of years, similar to the military with a certain amount of time and grade.

Then the unexpected happened. Two or three days after I started, I ended up in the emergency room needing emergency surgery. I had to call the partner I worked for to let him know I'd just been admitted to the hospital for further testing. What they found after giving me an internal scan with iodine was that I needed to have my gallbladder removed. Unknown to me, this would mark the beginning of significant health problems that would go on for years. A month after the test I lost 25 pounds which I could not afford, especially given my height. After numerous doctors' visits, we found the iodine was enough to push my thyroid into hyperthyroidism. I was diagnosed with Graves' disease and as they searched for a treatment that would work, I suffered joint, muscle, and eye pain, hair, and memory loss, fatigue, and several other symptoms that affected my daily actions. This went on for almost two years before I was able to get the disease affecting my immune system under control. It took so long because we found that I was allergic to several of the medications, which made it more difficult to treat. In many cases, I could not put a complete sentence together orally or in writing. This ultimately impacted my role with the firm and seemed to be one of the underlying causes of me not making manager the first time up. Basically, I was told that I was illiterate and not doing the job as a team lead.

The initial two years at the firm were somewhat touch-and-go for two reasons. First, I did not realize how precise they wanted you to be with your grade point average. I had also listed my grade point average for the courses that I transferred to University of Maryland

University College which were part of my courses for my masters. Since I hadn't fully decided to continue courses there, I was not listed as degree-seeking. In the workplace environment to which I'd become accustomed, asking employees their grade point average was not the norm; I was just thankful to have finished my degree while working multiple jobs. But eventually, my GPA emerged as an issue with human resources. My integrity was called into question and I was trying to understand if my grade point average was more important than my job experience. So I was six months in and there was the potential that I was going to be let go for lying on my job application. I understand their reasoning now but at the time, I had no clue that my GPA had to be absolutely accurate and my enrollment status for my graduate program totally set on my job application. If you hadn't worked in this type of organization before, you wouldn't understand the requirement. Thankfully, the issue was resolved and I was able to move on without it being held over my head.

The second issue was my health, which plagued me for several years as it went spiraling out of control and affected my everyday ability. I did not realize how serious it was until I saw the *Gail Devers Story*. Devers was an Olympic champion who was also diagnosed with Graves' disease. I was experiencing the same symptoms and was concerned when she also almost had to have her feet amputated because of the swelling. *Could this happen to me?* One time soon after, I had to take my PT test and my first sergeant and one of my admin NCO's had to help me off the track after my run. My legs and feet were noticeably swollen; it was almost like you could pop them with a pin. After seeing Gail's movie, I knew I had to get serious and made the decision to undergo the same treatment she did.

During my first assessment for manager at the firm, I did not make it. I was told there were several reasons for the rejection, one of them being that I was not working the same amount of hours as the people on my team for whom I had to set the example. The second reason was because my communication skills were not sufficient. To underscore the point, my partner pulled out one email I had sent him during the time I was coping with medical issues – something I never explained to him. He employed this one email as an example of my illiteracy and disqualification for the promotion. Needless to say, this was a significant blow. My response was that I might as well have been told to bend over and enjoy it. *Yes, I know.* Not appropriate, but that was the way I was feeling – incredibly betrayed and certain that someone was out to get me. As for my hours, what they did not take into account was that I was in the office every morning between 6:00 - 6:30 because I needed to pick up my child from daycare before 5:00 in the evening. So while many of them did not get to the office until 9:00, I already had been at my desk working for three hours. I mentioned before that I am an early bird who prefers to get a jump on the day to ensure I'm prepared and complete every necessary task on that day's agenda.

What they also did not take into account was that my team was from out of town which meant they did not have any responsibility in the evenings. They could stay at work longer and go to dinner together. All of these events resulted in me not making manager that year but I remained determined that this would not hold me back and if necessary, I would leave the firm. So I did what I do best: I worked with the human resources lead and the diversity lead and put together an action plan with them. I was embarrassed by the thought that they were saying I was illiterate based on one email but even though I knew it was wrong, there was no use fighting it. Instead, I took a grammar course as part of my action plan. I also worked on my health since that was the biggest source of my problems.

What are my key takeaways from the experience? First, you should never assume anything regarding expectations; you should clarify early and often to make sure you are all on the same sheet of music. Secondly, when something impacts your health and by extension, your overall functioning, seek treatment immediately instead of blowing it off. Lastly, relationships are critical to success in your business career and personal life. You need to build relationships at all levels within the work environment and sometimes your peers can be extremely important. While I eventually got over this whole mess, it bothered me for the longest time. So my final lesson is if you can't control it, just release it and move on.

Changing The Corporate Culture

As a result of expectations, I was told that only one of the team leads could be supported for promotion the next year and that I was the one selected to roll off the project. Well, disappointment flowed through me again but it was one of the best things that could have happened to me even though I did not know it at the time. I went to work for another partner who eventually became the chief operation officer for the whole firm. Just as before, I performed well but this time, it was recognized. I was supported by not only my project lead but the client lead, initiating the creation of a highly successful career. I went on to not only lead project teams but win contracts based on relationships I had developed in the business. I landed several key accounts even though I did not make partner until much later.

As a matter of fact, I worked for several partners who were instrumental to my success. In many cases, some were the total opposite of me; these are the projects that fostered the most professional growth. I was challenged in every way imaginable and seeing development in unexpected areas. My dedication and diligence eventually paid off: I made partner while I was on my first deployment in Kosovo and then returned home to become the Army client account lead. This was remarkable because my military career helped catapult me forward in my civilian career at a critical time. It is the integration and synchronization of the two that made all the difference in the world. I thought the deployment would derail my career but in reality, it did not.

Now I will say that the second deployment came at a time when I needed to take a break from the firm. I had taken on another role after being the Army account lead for several years to being the pseudo lead for another account with a prospective client. I was personally asked to do this in conjunction with taking on the role of Diversity Lead for our Federal business. While this should have been another highlight assignment, one of the individuals with whom I had to work closely jumped off the tracks in an extremely negative way. I have never ever felt threatened or uncomfortable in the work environment. And until I started collaborating with this gentleman, we'd enjoyed a compatible professional relationship. But as the business development lead for the account, he held firmly to his own vision, which differed significantly from mine. From the outset, it was clear that our opposing views as to how things should happen would create nothing but friction and conflict.

It had gotten to the point where I was told I was not to have a client meeting without him and should not be making any calls to the client at all. This was problematic because I also had sales and revenue goals I needed to meet. I knew I was in trouble and tried to deal with it as best as I could. It was also during this time that I was nominated by the firm for a fellowship with the International Women's Leadership Association. I should have been feeling as if I was on the top of the world but instead, I wanted to run and hide. I was beginning to hate showing up for work every day and it took all the strength I could muster to continue to support a partner for whom I'd truly wanted to work and a business development lead for whom I'd lost respect. When the second deployment became a reality, I welcomed it for many reasons. I feared I might snap and quit one day but felt that I should not let someone run me out of an organization I loved just as much as I loved wearing the uniform.

So I deployed to Afghanistan in 2011 as part of the Afghanistan national security forces team.

Upon returning from the deployment, I had some trouble transitioning back to work. It was harder to reconnect with people and get back to my overall routine. I think this was in part due to a lack of a defined role, organizational changes, and other stressful factors including an office move. When I returned to work, I had to report to a new and unfamiliar office. It took about three- to- four months to obtain a role that started out as temporary and ended up lasting two-and-a-half years. While I was not overly excited about the role initially, I gained valuable experience and discovered I was really good at being a commercial director focusing on business operations within a portfolio. I ultimately got my groove back, started mentoring and coaching others, and re-engaged with diversity activities. This role prepared me for a larger and broader assignment as a director of operations for an operating unit. When I was asked if I would be interested, I knew that this would be a good stretch role that would significantly challenge me in numerous ways – again, developing new relationships, understanding the business at a much broader level, and working with leadership to define and implement strategic organizational changes. It was definitely the highlight of my consulting career, a role that many work diligently to achieve.

When I think back over my career, my military and civilian roles have weaved in and out of each other in many cases seamlessly but at other times in direct conflict. Ironically, it also represents how I have felt about myself on any given day. There were times when I knew clearly who I was, where I was going, and what I wanted. But there have been other times when I would look in the mirror and experience self-doubt. I am sure many will say that you never really find your true self – the self you enjoy, the self you are comfortable being, and the self that is full of confidence and swagger. No matter how self-assured one may seem, there may still be the slightest feeling of doubt or the presence of the little monster that rears its ugly head from time to time. It is during those times that you need to reflect on your past in order to move forward to the future. You must call upon every bit of yourself. You need to know that you are worthy, valued, and needed. Until you become comfortable in your own skin and unafraid to show the world who you are, the inner you has not yet emerged or even been born. This is what helps you to rise above the fray of everything else: to knock the monster of self-doubt off your shoulder and be happy with just being you. After all else, I have emerged.

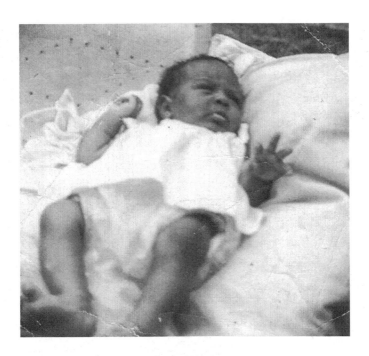

Me as a baby

My Beautiful Mother

Me Riding a Bike

With my cousin at my Godmothers House

With my uncles Merritt and Hammond

Pop-pop in the U.S. Navy

Doing what I loved best: playing basketball with my uncles

My great-grandmother, whom I called Grandma

Me in the Second Grade (left) and Third Grade (right)

My grandparents little house in the Maryland countryside

Afghanistan, January 2012, assisting with Operation Outreach

Afghanistan, January 2012, assisting with Operation Outreach

Afghanistan, January 2012, assisting with Operation Outreach

Me with Afghanistan General Mohammadzai

Our beautiful Hindu Vow Renewal Ceremony my husband Raj and daughters Shaniece and Tara (Photo Credit: Kirth Bobb Photography)

My daughters Shaniece and Tara surround me at our Hindu Vow Renewal Ceremony (Photo Credit: Kirth Bobb Photography)

Holding a press conference around Day 3 of the Baltimore riots

Governor's Installation – with Governor and First Lady Hogan
and Lt. Governor and Mrs. Rutherford

Camp Pendleton Drivers' Training

Speaking/moderating at the Institute for Veterans and Military Families, accompanied by Retired Commander Sergeant Major Cynthia Pritchett

CHAPTER 7

RELATIONSHIPS AND MENTORING:
BUILDING A SUPPORT SYSTEM

As I have discussed, when I was growing up there was always plenty of family around. Up until the time I turned nine and was taken from my grandparents' home, I saw my married uncles and aunts every weekend and sometimes during the week. I thoroughly enjoyed these visits, which meant I also got to spend time with my cousins. Oftentimes some of them would take me home for weekends and holidays, and even to special events. From a young age, I learned the value and joy of being part of a large family.

Sadly, after the age of nine, I did not get to see most of them as often thanks to my parents. As a child and adolescent, these perceived family feuds were just too daunting to deal with even though they had nothing to do with me. Still, just the thought of getting into trouble with my mother or father for talking to forbidden family members was enough to stop me from reaching out to them. This is a burden no adult – and certainly no parent – should ever place on an innocent child's shoulders.

However, my parents did retain a few close relationships with extended family, among them Uncle Jerome and Aunt Nancy, who were around the most. Aunt Nancy was one of my mom's best friends and whenever she came over with my uncle it gave us a sense of freedom. In her presence, my mom was always in a good mood. I loved when they spent the night because Mom would fix breakfast in the morning for all of us and it was just like a great big family gathering. Aunt Nancy brought out the best in my mother and maintained a unique relationship with her during those years, one that no one else had.

Uncle Jerome used to pick me up on Fridays and bring me back on Saturdays and sometimes Sundays, offering a much-needed getaway during the part of my youth spent in my parents' home. Uncle Wayne and Aunt Charlotte, who lived next door to us, were always there to support me even when circumstances made it difficult for them. When I had no way of obtaining basic necessities like sanitary products, Aunt Charlotte consistently came through for me. When I was told I was not allowed to visit next door, it was tough because I truly appreciated their kindness and generosity. I could always count on talking to my aunts about life and the challenges I faced at home; they would encourage me to do the best I could. They assured me my parents loved me and everything would be okay. Regardless of how badly my mother and father treated them, they never retaliated with a bad or unkind word. I simply could not understand how they could be this loving and tolerant, even when on the receiving end of such vindictive behavior. I remember how much I wished my mother could understand that while we were all individuals with our own special qualities and idiosyncrasies, we were still family. Even in the most troubling times, my siblings and I loved our relatives the only way we were permitted: from a distance.

Making a Difference: Teachers and Coaches

During my high school years, I had a love for school mainly because it was a place where I could be myself. Earlier I talked about my passion for basketball above all other sports, something instilled in me from an early age when I first learned how to dribble and shoot. The exhilarating feeling of being in control on the basketball court no doubt fed my love of the game which I continued to play right up until I left school.

The funny thing about living in a rural area is that while we don't live close by, we all seem to know one another. My basketball coach worked with many of my uncles since we all went to the same school. He was not always the basketball coach; I think he also coached soccer, track and maybe even football at one point in time. I'm not sure if he was ever formally recognized for his decades of contributions to the school or if he even understood the extent to which he positively impacted our lives, especially mine.

Coach Bob Dawson was an exceptional person who genuinely cared about his players and students. He took an interest in me and recognized my potential. While I did anything I could to play basketball, most of the time I would stay after school with no idea as to how I was going to get home. Coach Dawson always gave me a ride after practice, regardless of the time. If I did not have a ride to practice on the weekends, he would pick me up and take me back home even though he lived 40 minutes away in the opposite direction. Yet he never seemed to mind. One year when my parents refused to let me play, he came over to the house and convinced them to let me stay on the team. I never knew how lucky I was to have him both as a coach and a mentor who truly cared about my future.

After I had left home in the aftermath of my mother's backlash against me regarding the rape, he continued to pick me up, this time, to take me to school. Because I didn't want to burden him with my problems, I never told him what was going on. I remember his reaction when I informed him about my plan to leave Linganore to transfer to another high school that was closer to work since I needed the money: Coach Dawson offered to hire me to do odds-and-ends jobs for him so I could still play for the team and continue my education. Once again, his kindness amazed me but I declined his offer because I believed I was too much of a burden on this man who'd already gone above and beyond the call of duty on my behalf.

While we had our share of phenomenal teachers, one, in particular, is memorable: Mrs. Kline. I supported her as a teacher's aide and developed a close relationship with her in the ninth and tenth grades when I helped her during my free period. That's when we would talk about everything. There were days I recall crying in her office as she prayed with me, consoled me, and spoke words of encouragement to me. An absolutely incredible woman, Mrs. Kline had several children of her own going to the school yet always took the time to listen to me. Her genuine expressions of affection and concern made me wish she could be my mother. When life at home took a turn for the worse, she offered to take me in; we talked about how she would convert her sewing room into a bedroom in exchange for doing chores around the house, which was not a big deal for me. She even talked to my mother and told her she wanted me to come live with them, resulting in my mother cussing her out before hanging up the phone. Of course, the incident also got me into trouble for "telling lies" as my mother put it.

Thankfully, this ugly incident did not shake up our friendship and I continued to dream about living with her. Whether because it never occurred to me or I was just too embarrassed, I never did seek out Mrs. Kline when I finally left home with no place to go. Looking back, I realize we as humans tend to underrate relationships: we have no concept of their value and power. As a vulnerable teenager, I know I didn't. But now I recognize that multiple people come in and out of our lives for various reasons. I consider these encounters to be blessings and/or signs from God; it is fate at work and it is up to us to understand the purpose of every interaction.

Triniman

Fate seems to take care of everything – even when what you think you want is not what is best for you. As I mentioned previously, I met the man who would become my husband in a nightclub. We seemed to hit it off right away. A native of Trinidad, he was interesting and unlike any man I'd met before. As we talked that first night, he told me all about his home country and his family but what I loved most about our conversation was the fact that he was so easy to talk to. He told me he was going to college while working full-time – a clear indication he had goals, aspirations, and a good head on his shoulders.

On that first night and over the course of the next several months he took me out, mostly for meals; I couldn't tell if he thought I was too skinny or if he liked to eat. Although we began to see each other more frequently, we still had not shared even a single kiss. I knew he liked me but couldn't figure out whether he was inexperienced or disinterested in women. Several months after our meeting at the club, Valentine's Day rolled around. Our plans included dinner with my sister and her husband at their place. Prior to the gathering, I told my sister I wasn't sure if this guy even liked me because he was oddly distant when it came to romance. Together we devised a plan to ensure that the evening's festivities would help me determine if he liked me or not – with the hope that maybe he would kiss me for Valentine's Day. The four of us had a wonderful time and when he and I returned to my apartment, he came in and presented me with the gift of a beautiful, delicate gold ankle bracelet.

As he got up to leave, I walked him to the door, confident there was no way he'd go without at least giving me a goodnight kiss. Frustrated when he didn't make a move, I decided to take matters into my own hands and kissed him. Well, I don't know if he perceived my gesture as too forward, a mistake, or an unwelcomed advance because while he kissed me back, he nearly broke down my door trying to get out!

All I could surmise was that this guy had to be completely inexperienced; I just wasn't sure how I could or would move forward with him. Over the subsequent weeks, I noticed a change in his behavior where he was a little more romantic, but not much. After about another month following an outing at the club, we came back to my place, where he stayed part of the night. Talk about *fast forward.* I finally got a chance to see his license and his side profile photo told me more than I wanted to know – namely that he was younger than 21 years old. *Oh my God, I had no idea because when we met he told me he was 25 and I believed him.* Our ensuing conversation revealed he was definitely younger than 21, which mortified and concerned me: he was much too unworldly for my liking. While we did go out a few more times, I started to distance myself from him, avoiding phone calls and circumstances where we'd likely run into each other. In March of that year, I cut off all contact and informed my sister I had no interest in being in a relationship with someone this innocent. Her response? This was a big mistake on my part because up to this point, with perhaps one notable exception, all of the other guys I'd dated had proven to be losers.

Regardless, I ignored her advice and continued to play the field. I had many ups and downs but no luck in finding someone who would make a good companion no matter how hard I tried. You know what they say when you are looking for something, you are not likely to find it. But when you least expect it, you are more likely to find what you are not looking for. At summer's end, my sister and I had a conversation about my unhappiness. I complained I was tired of being alone but would not settle for less. She suggested I give Raj another try because he was smart and fun to be with. What I didn't know at the time but would ultimately discover is that I was his first real girlfriend.

Second Chances: Reconsidering My Options

The more I thought about it, the more I appreciated the value of going out with a guy who didn't have issues from all of the previous women he'd dated. It was an appealing proposition: at just three years older, I'd already amassed a lifetime of issues for the both of us. Maybe this relationship would be worth it in the long run. With all of this in mind, one evening I decided to give him a call. When he asked if I would like to go out, I said yes without hesitation. I'll always remember the hilarious comedy of errors that characterized the evening.

When we got into the car, he put on a pair of one-armed glasses that were taped in the middle. Of course, I had to ask him why he didn't just buy a new pair but he brushed it off by saying the glasses had recently broken and he hadn't had time to shop for new ones. On the way to dinner we stopped at a gas station to fill the tank but before he got out to pump, he proceeded to pull all kinds of change and money from under his car mat. I was beginning to wonder if I'd made the right choice because I'd never experienced anything like this before on a date. Between scraping change from under his car mat and driving around in damaged glasses, I began to doubt he had any money. Yet he did take me to dinner at least once a week.

During this "second phase" of our relationship, I made another interesting discovery: the gas gauge on his car barely worked, which sometimes meant he would run out. One night while waiting for him to come over, he called to inform me he needed me to bring him some gas – and hurry. I replied, "Why on earth did you run out of gas and why should I hurry?" He explained he was stuck in a bad part of DC and feared it might not be a good idea to hang out there much longer. Worried for his safety, I advised him to stay put with the condition to give me some time. After bundling up my daughter Shaniece (who slept soundly throughout the ordeal), we went to pick him up. At least once every two weeks we'd replay this scenario, which annoyed me to no end. However, to make up for the inconvenience and express his gratitude, he would occasionally send me flowers at work. I'd reciprocate by bringing him dinner once in a while since he worked crazy, long hours. After leaving the food in his car, I'd head back home.

One day I dropped him off at work and on the way to pick him up later, his car ran out of gas just as I was about to pull into the station. Mind you, I had already asked him about the fuel situation and he'd assured me the car had plenty of juice. Well, I questioned his definition of the word "plenty" since it seemed the vehicle could never keep a full tank. Thankfully, I was able to push the car to the pump to fill up but I did let him have it on that one. To this day, even though he never runs out of gas he will drive until he is riding on fumes. I am not sure what his infatuation is with taking a chance on the road; it still drives me crazy.

Culture Clash and Unconscious Bias

Gasoline problems aside, it seemed we were both ready to make a go of this relationship the second time around and we soon became a "hot item." We spent as much time together as we could even with our grueling school and work schedules. Because I also had parental responsibilities, it was tough to keep things separate until I was sure we would be dating longer term. At work, many of my friends were unsupportive; all they could see was that he was of Indian descent, which in their minds meant he came from a stereotypical culture in which women were disrespected. They warned me I'd have to walk ten steps behind him and get used to being treated as an inferior because I was a woman; this relationship could never work because women and men are held to different standards. Keep in mind, none of them had actually dated someone from Raj's culture; they simply accepted the stereotypes they'd heard about as truth.

As I listened, the only thought running through my mind was, *how was that any different from what I'd already experienced in the workplace?* I already knew about the disparities between men and women: I dealt with it on a daily basis and handled it well. While I appreciated their well-intentioned (if misguided) advice, I took a leap of faith, trusting God had a plan for me in this department.

Although Raj lived with his brother and a few other family members, I did not meet them for quite a while, a choice that was best for everyone involved. However, his relatives wanted to know all about the woman who was dominating his time. In those days we did not have cell phones; using the land line for communication was our only option, which meant I was either calling his house or he was calling mine. Still I did meet Raj's nephew Barry, who lived with them. We became good friends even though I got the distinct impression he felt he would be a better match for me. Instinctively, I made sure Barry and I stayed in the *friend lane*, even going so far as to fix him up with a friend of mine so we could double date. Eventually, he turned out to be a solid, dependable guy; I am genuinely thankful for the platonic relationship we developed and his willingness to listen and talk with me when I needed a confidant.

My friendship with Barry marked the extent of my meaningful interactions with Raj's family until the day he asked me to attend a presentation party. When I accepted, I had no clue what this event entailed but later discovered my boyfriend played on a cricket team; they were getting together to distribute awards at another teammate's home. I remember walking through the door and into a large gathering of people who watched the two of us intently. Naturally I was somewhat uncomfortable because I did not know anyone. But soon several guys asked me to dance. As I politely obliged, I was astounded by some of their inappropriate comments: here I was, Raj's date – as evidenced by the fact I'd shown up for the party on his arm – and a few of his friends tried to convince me I should dump him to be with one of them. I'll admit, I wasn't sure if I looked too old for him or if they truly felt an attraction. Regardless of their motives, it was definitely a bit unnerving for me and somewhat arrogant of them. But aside from this unfortunate incident, it was a great party and my first foray into the Trini scene. While I thoroughly enjoyed myself, I was ready to leave when the time came. Looking back, what I liked the most was that they were all carefree and fun-loving people.

One day, Raj called me at work to ask for a favor, an unusual occurrence because he never asked me to do anything for him. Apparently, a few of his family members needed jobs and he thought I could help them since I worked security in the evenings.

Since they'd just relocated from Trinidad, I took them out to look for employment not realizing that these three men were Raj's brothers-in-law and family friends. Over the course of a few different days, I took some time off from work to take these friendly, funny guys to a number of places. By now I had purchased another car and had no idea what to do with my old clunker so I asked Raj if they would like to use it; while it wasn't fancy at least it would provide them with transportation. They gratefully accepted my offer and I allowed them to use the car until it just would not go any longer. While I couldn't afford much in those days, I continued to pay for the insurance to keep them covered while driving around. I figured they were doing me a favor because I'd been trying to decide what to do with the old junker anyway. Although I saw this as a small gesture on my part, I had no idea the extent to which my actions had made an impact on them. Even though I tried to help them professionally, I was unfamiliar with their skills and experience in the construction industry. We did go to a few sites but two of them ended up getting jobs with one of the large construction companies on their own.

Acceptance Is a Two-Way Street

Raj and I continued to date and throughout the next year, I got to meet more of his family and friends. His family reminded me of mine in my early years: they were all so very close and genuinely enjoyed being around one another. Raj is from a family of eight, two sisters and five brothers. Up to this point, I had only met three of his brothers and one sister as our relationship became pretty steady. I don't remember how often we saw each other but we talked every day. When we'd progressed to a level where I felt fairly comfortable, I introduced him to my daughter Shaniece, who was about four or five when we started dating. They'd never been formally introduced since she'd slept through the "rescue mission" the day he ran out of gas on his way to my apartment. No, I wasn't looking for someone to be her father but at the same time, I didn't want to subject her to someone who wouldn't treat her well.

As for Raj, we engaged in several discussions about our individual family dynamics. Since I was not Trinidadian, he warned me that his family may not be as accepting even though his brother was in an interracial marriage. Proactively, we talked about how we would handle his family's reaction. Well as it turned out, it did not really become an issue with those whom I'd already met, possibly because of my personality and outlook on life. I love people and I found Raj's folks to be so wonderful that I just enjoyed being in their company. I didn't worry about what they might be thinking about me and frankly didn't care.

Still, I experienced moments of discomfort when surrounded by his family and friends who talked among themselves about things I had no knowledge of. To navigate through these situations, I made an honest effort to keep an open mind, respect their culture, and recognize that my family did the same thing when we were all together. This positive attitude paid dividends for me in terms of being able to integrate with them without any real or perceived problems. We were forthright and honest in discussing my race, my status as a single parent, and other important aspects of my life; therefore, none of these things ever became a looming issue just waiting to blow up.

While that provided an excellent foundation, we continued to make it a habit of talking over anything resembling a potentially damaging problem. Now that was easier said than done because during this time, Raj went to visit his family in Canada for about a week – or so he told me. When he decided to stay longer, he didn't even bother to tell me. When I'd call his house they'd just say he wasn't back yet. I am sure they probably thought, *who is this crazy girl calling him all the time?* One day when I called, his nephew, Shane answered the phone and told me he went to visit his old girlfriend. Since this was news to me, I flipped. When Raj finally returned several weeks later, he thought what Shane did was funny but I didn't see anything humorous about it. Angrily, I informed him I was not going to be in a relationship with him if he refused to communicate. Yes, our communication at times left something to be desired.

Even after I expressed my anger and frustration over his little disappearing act, he'd still run off to hang out with the guys in the family, visiting with them for days at a time. Whenever he took off without a word, they would cover by telling me he either wasn't there or was sick in bed. I never understood what the deal was until much later when I watched him interact with his family. As our relationship developed, he pulled these stunts less frequently. But in the early years, his behavior was a little nerve-wracking; I am surprised I even put up with it but somehow I did.

After we'd been together for several years, I won an all-expenses paid trip for four to Disney World in Florida. At this stage in our courtship, Raj came over often but never stayed the night because he lived with his brother and wanted to be respectful to ensure he was not taking advantage of the situation. Naturally, when I invited him to come along with us on our trip he declined; he wouldn't go out of respect for his brother and what they might think.

Since my daughter had pet hamsters and fish, I asked Raj to take care of them for us until we returned – unaware that he not only disliked furry animals, he was downright terrified of them. He wouldn't touch them at all. When we got back from Disney, our hamsters were dead but our fish were still alive. When I asked if he fed them, he replied, "You expected me to put my hand in the cage with those things?" I informed him he owed Shaniece new hamsters since he essentially let them starve to death.

As for the trip, one of my girlfriends and her son went with us. Thank goodness it was all expenses paid because I didn't have much money for extras. In fact, this was the first and only real vacation I'd taken my daughter on since she was born. In those days, "vacation" for me entailed taking off of one job in order to work another. And although I respected Raj's decision, I wished he would have gone with us. Still, we enjoyed ourselves immensely.

Deeper Than a Biological Bond

He continued to be a steady friend and partner who proved the depth of his love for us in the aftermath of a frightening incident that occurred later on. I'd been living in a rented condo off of Indian Head Highway in Oxon Hill Maryland when Raj and I decided to go out for a late evening on the DC waterfront. We hired a babysitter who lived in our neighborhood to take care of my child. She was about 16 or 17 years old and often played with her in the playground area. I had employed her a few times, especially right after school for Shaniece, who enjoyed spending time with her.

We'd just arrived at the event when I got a call on my cell informing me I needed to get home right away; someone had broken into the condo from the balcony. Panicked, we left immediately before even having a chance to enjoy the evening.

When we got home, the police were still there. Evidently the person had entered through the small window from the balcony but when they apprehended him he claimed he entered the wrong unit. However, his story didn't jive with the girls' version of events. They told us they'd yelled at him to go away but he still came in. That's when they ran into my bedroom, locked the door, and hid in my closet behind the clothes. Shaniece had pulled the phone along with her to call 911. They yelled at him that the police were on their way and finally heard him run out the door.

What stands out most in my mind about that harrowing night was Raj's insistence on sleeping over to keep us safe since we had nowhere else to go. Soon after, he informed me I had to move out of there – a statement of the obvious. As I worked on finding another place to live in a more secure neighborhood, a realization struck me: I'd been living here when I found out my brother had molested my daughter, even though it had taken place at our previous residence. Raj had been my rock through all of that ugliness and here he was once again supporting me through yet another ordeal. Without a doubt, it was crystal-clear he was my best friend and confidant.

We found a nicer place to rent in a better location in the Oxon Hill area, where we remained for a few years. In our new home, we had wonderful neighbors and plenty of kids for Shaniece to play with. The folks who lived upstairs watched her for me when I had to work late or had plans to go out with Raj. However, while my daughter and I enjoyed this peaceful living arrangement, I also dealt with a few troubling spots in my relationship.

Déjà vu: Alcohol and Anger

Raj and I had become one of the well-known couples at Classics, a fixture there on either a Friday or Saturday evening (not both) every weekend. By now we were comfortable with our relationship but one night something happened between us; something I cannot even recall in detail. All I remember is having too much to drink and arguing excessively – to the point where my neighbor paid me a visit the next day to ensure everything was alright.

I didn't think he'd consumed much because he was not a heavy drinker. However, he did have some Remy, which was an unusual choice for him. When we arrived back at my place that night, I asked him to leave, which seemed to make him go crazy. He started throwing objects around and knocking over my plants, causing me to run into my bedroom and lock the door. In tears, I called his brother to come and get him, terrified he was going to break down my bedroom door. That night, I knew we had to make some much-needed changes for the sake of our relationship.

At that moment, I flashed back to my parents. What had occurred between Raj and me was a painful reminder of what used to happen when my mother and father went out. Having been forced to deal with their volatile behavior as a child and teen, I resolved to spare my daughter from the same kind of pain: there was no way I wanted her to sit by and watch me deal with this kind of abuse. Luckily she was not there that night. I cried myself to sleep wondering what to do as I thought all of the years we'd already spent together just circling the drain. *Is this how it was going to end?* I surely didn't want to break up but if we were going to stay together, we both needed to agree that our behavior had to change.

Neither of us wanted a tumultuous relationship. While we understood as human beings we were going to disagree and even argue at times, we recognized our error in allowing this kind of escalation. Our desire to nurture our relationship compelled us to take a new course of action. We started by going to the club less frequently in favor of activities like hanging out with the family, which was always uplifting. As an added bonus, time spent with family meant we didn't have to handle the random hurtful comments from other guys about us in reference to Raj's race. Whenever I heard one of them call him a derogatory name like "wetback" I would see red: just because I was not with a black man did not mean they could disrespect him or me. While Raj's response was to keep quiet, I would invariably comment back. Thankfully, nothing like this has happened in a long time. People are much more accepting in the area in which we now live and I'm glad we no longer have to be subjected to such prejudice.

We moved forward in a positive direction, even discussing the possibility of having a child together and expanding our family. Even though Shaniece was not his biological daughter, Raj was protective of her. One year around Christmas, my ex-husband was supposed to visit her. This concerned Raj, who didn't want him to be alone with her somewhere in case he decided to run off with her to parts unknown. When it appeared he was wavering about flying up to Maryland because of a lack of money, Raj even offered to let him stay with us for the duration of his visit. The fact that this man would allow my ex to stay in our home is a testament to his character; we were even going to pick him up from the airport. Well, when the scheduled day arrived – I don't recall whether it was Christmas Eve or Christmas Day – John called me early in the morning to announce he wasn't coming after all.

For a man who blamed me for his misfortune after I divorced him and got full custody, he did not even make serious attempts to spend time with his daughter. Angered by his latest stunt, I discussed the possibility of suing him for child support with Raj, who told me we didn't need it because he would take care of Shaniece. From that point on he supported her every need and never questioned whether or not she should have something, even though we were not married. Yet he never once complained about providing for her.

As she grew, Shaniece came to look upon Raj as her father – the man she could rely on, the man who proved by his actions that fatherhood transcended biology. In our case, it also transcended legal adoption, though when she turned eighteen, she petitioned the court to officially change her last name to Singh. She did this all on her own in an act of gratitude and love for Raj – her father in every way that mattered.

Partnering for Success

Right around the time Raj freely embraced the role of devoted dad to Shaniece, I decided to go to officer candidate school. Since Raj and I were both taking classes, we would cooperate with each other to make this arrangement work. The drill weekends for the school started on Friday nights and ended on Sundays, which meant I had to stay there all weekend. Raj was able to watch Shaniece for some of them but most weekends she stayed with one of my best friends whose children went to the same school. The arrangement strengthened the kids' close friendships and during the times Shaniece stayed with them they treated her like a sister.

For the duration of officer candidate school, I made a variety of gestures to support the team, like getting our helmets ready for the "black phase" which would take place before our final two weeks. In a demonstration of support, Raj helped me with sanding down the helmets, then painting and putting a high gloss on them. He accompanied me to events without complaint. By the time graduation neared we'd been dating for about five or six years. He'd nearly moved in all of his belongings so we decided to make it official and I gave him a key. When I resolved I would not move out of my place for any guy, I meant it. If we were going to live together, I would be in the driver's seat, meaning if the relationship broke up the guy would be the one to get out of *my* home.

But after enduring both good and bad times, he remained by my side even though he had not yet made any move to propose. When I left for my branch qualification school, we decided to move out to Waldorf where we found a beautiful townhouse for rent in a desirable neighborhood. Knowing Shaniece would live a good area put my mind at ease. While at school, I started thinking more and more about our future and subsequently informed Raj I did not think we should stay together if we were not going to get married; after all, I was not getting any younger and wanted more kids. So I told him that he had a choice to make – but I never expected he would ask me to elope.

I came home for the Thanksgiving break and we secretly married at the courthouse two days after the holiday. We didn't share the news with anyone, agreeing to plan a wedding for the following summer after Raj told his parents in person. When I returned for good, I accepted a better job offer and we started talking about having a child together. One particular weekend at his sister's house, he was in rare form: in front of the whole group, he got down on his knees and asked me to marry him. Even though we were already husband and wife as evidenced by the ring I was wearing, he explained he wanted to do this the right way; the way he wanted it to happen. Although stunned, I, of course, did not say no. We'd already been partying it up and his marriage proposal gave us another reason to celebrate. Soon after, we decided I would go off of birth control, agreeing that if I got pregnant before the wedding, it wouldn't be a big deal since we were in the process of setting a date.

During his parents' visit in May of 1992, Raj broke the news of our impending marriage. Although we'd assumed the worst, they told him all they wanted was his happiness. Afterward, he arranged for me to meet them. Although cordial during the visit, they seemed quiet and reserved which made it difficult for me to figure out what they were thinking. Still, it was a relief to have everything out in the open so we could start making plans for our July 18 nuptials – an event we had no clue how to finance, notwithstanding the fact we were both employed full time.

Well, things have a way of working out because Raj's brother and his wife offered to host our reception at their home as a wedding present. When they asked how we envisioned it, I described an occasion where folks could just let their hair down and have fun. Then there was the discussion as to what kind of marriage ceremony we preferred. While I would have loved to have planned something elaborate, in the end, we decided on a simple Christian wedding. Now the challenge was finding someone to marry us. You see, Raj is a Hindu and I am a Christian. My church turned us down for two reasons: first they wanted him to convert and second, they would not do renewals since technically we were already married. The ensuing discussions with the church about his religion left me with a sour taste in my mouth because I believe we are all God's children regardless of how or to whom we pray. If I wasn't asking him to convert, why should they? I felt strongly about my position, especially since he and I had been making our relationship work for years. That was the last time I ever went to that church even though I was a member.

On my girlfriend's recommendation, I talked to the Chaplain on Andrews Air Force Base, who agreed to marry us as long as we attended counseling sessions with him. We accepted the deal and in the process, he came to the conclusion we were made for one another. He was intrigued by our ability to successfully intertwine our two culturally divergent backgrounds. Having solved the issues pertaining to the ceremony, I turned my attention to finding a dress but in spite of hours spent shopping I couldn't find anything I truly liked. In my mind I envisioned flowing chiffon – similar to a saree but not exactly – and I came up empty. One day my girlfriend offered me her dress and after I saw it in person, I realized the bodice would have to be re-laced. It was hard to believe she was willing to let go of such a beautiful gown but my friend told me I could have it. She'd been incredibly good to me over the years and this was just the latest example of her generosity. I tried to pay her but she wouldn't hear of it. It cost a negligible amount of money to replace the lace, which was done by a co-worker from the furniture store. Once settled on my own gown, I set about the business of finding dresses for my small bridal party.

One of my best friends was my matron of honor. Earlier I told the story of the older gentleman I'd dated at a time in my life when I desperately needed to meet a chivalrous man. That relationship brought a multitude of blessings into my life, including a meaningful friendship with his sister, with whom I'd remained close over the years. I owed much to her.

I chose royal blue and white as my color scheme. Since I did not want real flowers, I made all of the arrangements myself, including the lapel flowers. Shaniece was my flower girl, Raj's brother was his best man, his nephews were ushers, and his youngest nephew was our ring bearer. As our plans came together, I reached out to my dad with the request to walk me down the aisle. I don't remember the whole conversation but in the end, he declined and neither of my parents even came to my wedding. With no one to escort me on my special day, I didn't know what I was going to do. Reflecting back on it now, I should have asked one of my uncles but instead asked another friend with whom I had grown close over the years. We'd worked together at the furniture store and attended the same church. A wonderful man and mentor, he felt honored to walk me down the aisle since he felt like I was his daughter anyway.

Amid the flurry of wedding preparations, I became concerned because I'd been off birth control for a good while yet had not gotten pregnant. I went to the doctor, who ordered a series of tests that determined there would be no way for me to conceive, carry, and deliver another baby without surgery. After giving birth to Shaniece I had contracted a staph infection and suffered one miscarriage; now it appeared both Fallopian tubes were blocked and I had tons of scar tissue. We decided to have the minimally invasive surgery only to discover that the scar tissue was so widespread they could not even remove it. Consequently, they scheduled me for a more invasive laparotomy. This surgery took almost three hours and required a recovery period of several weeks, which meant I'd be executing all of the wedding preparations while convalescing. Although the doctor felt absolutely confident the procedure would prove successful, only time would tell. Raj and I took a more detached approach: if it was meant to happen, it would.

When our wedding day arrived, we could only afford one limo, which we used to pick up and transport Raj and his family from Virginia to the chapel on Andrews, where I would meet up with them. After the ceremony, someone would drive my car to Virginia for the reception. Well, as I've said before, the best-laid plans often go awry; my angst-filled morning began with my car's refusal to start after I'd loaded everything into it, thanks to an intermittent electronic start issue. Naturally it had to act up on my wedding day and create unnecessary panic. As a result, I left about 30 minutes later than I should have to get to the chapel.

You may be wondering why I didn't call Raj for help. He had spent the night in Virginia to take part in the Hindu custom of preparing the groom for his wedding even though we were not having a Hindu ceremony. This ritual, known as the Haldi, involved the application of turmeric and oils to his skin the night before. Since I was not even remotely familiar with these customs, I had no idea what was involved and didn't want to worry him with the whole car situation. Besides, there were tons of people on his end getting ready; I felt it best not to add to the confusion.

The moment I arrived at the chapel I started to put myself together, with a little help from a few of my friends. When the ceremony time approached, the groom and family still had not arrived. As a matter of fact, in true Trini fashion, they were all 15 minutes late. *Talk about my nerves being shot.* All kinds of things went through my mind: *What if he just stood me up? What if they were not coming? Oh my God.* I did not know what I was going to do.

But once they arrived, I settled down and the ceremony

proceeded without incident. As I walked down the aisle, I couldn't believe that this stunningly handsome man was going to be my husband. After countless years of pain and heartache, it was difficult to comprehend that God had given me such a wonderful gift. Filled with overwhelming gratitude, my heart felt as if it would burst and I started to cry before the ritual even began. As a matter of fact, I'm not sure I *stopped* bawling before it ended. My beautiful ceremony was followed by an equally remarkable reception. It was a true Trini celebration and during our first dance my brother-in-law, to whom I'd given my old clunker years before, poured a bottle of what looked like vodka all over us and pretended to lick it off. What a way to join the family! Let's just say he is the fun and crazy one, which means you always have to expect the unexpected whenever he's around. I had never seen Raj enjoy himself as much as he did that night. It was magical.

After becoming husband and wife, we spent quality time with Raj's mom and sister, who would soon be returning to Trinidad. On the day of their departure, Raj called me at work and asked if I would stop by to see them before they left. His mom walked me out to my car as I was leaving and I could tell she was sad. That's when she told me she had a gift for me, a lovely gold bangle, which moved me to tears. When I embraced her warmly and promised I'd take excellent care of her baby, she began to weep. Little did I know, it would be the last time I'd ever see her.

Two Lives Taken, Another Given

Some months later, I came home from work sick. This pattern had been repeating itself for days, giving me the feeling that maybe, just *maybe* it was a sign and not something else. I decided to stop at the drug store for a pregnancy test kit, hoping I was not just coming down with something like the flu. To my surprise and delight, it was positive. Although elated by the results, I felt so awful I had to lay down for a while. When Raj arrived home, I was still asleep but he sat down beside me to ask if I was alright. I told him I was fine, just a little tired, but that I had something to tell him. With that, I pulled out the test stick and showed it to him. He looked at me with a slightly confused expression so I affirmed, "I am pregnant." As he absorbed the meaning of the words, he gave me a look of disbelief that seemed to ask, *are you messing with me?* After I assured him we were really going to have a baby, he started jumping up and down and shouting as if he'd just won the lottery. Given the physical problems the doctors had uncovered during my surgery, we thought this would never happen. We also knew we had a long road ahead but in that moment, we just basked in the joyful news.

Once I felt I was out of the danger zone I told the family. Shaniece was excited she was going to be a big sister. About three months in I lost my beloved grandmother, which was a huge blow. As for the pregnancy, I was sick for eight straight months but still worked every day. It became a running joke during lunch that the table nearest the bathroom would be reserved for me just in case. Those who knew me would wait to see if it was a good or bad day based on my ability to properly digest food. I kept a jar of peanut butter in my desk because it was one of the only things I could keep down. Every morning before leaving for the office I would eat a spoonful of Tamarind sauce that had been sent to us from Trinidad. It is usually enjoyed with different foods but for some reason, the spicy/sweet/tangy mixture eased my morning sickness.

Being sick constantly posed a problem in gaining weight but eventually all resolved itself; I lost ten pounds but then gained eighteen. As I mentioned before, we lost Ma about three weeks before I gave birth to a little girl. We named her after my sister-in-law who was living here in the US with whom I'd grown close. Since my mother-in-law's name was Baghmani, we added the initials for Ma in her name. In the Hindu culture, there are also names given by the pundit, which is similar to a priest. Our daughter received a combination of everything.

While I had the next four months off from work, we considered our childcare options in preparation for my return. We researched nannies and au pairs to figure out which direction we wanted to go. Everything was unbelievably expensive but staying home wasn't a possibility because we could not afford to lose income. One day as I was talking to my sister-in-law about it, she asked why would we hire someone when she could be the caretaker. It was a marvelous idea; however, we didn't want to inconvenience her. In the end, it was an offer we couldn't refuse and she took care of our little one for a number of years until we thought she was ready for a day school.

Serendipitously, the day school we enrolled her in was located in the same neighborhood where my sister-in-law lived. What a blessing to know if we were running late, or if they just wanted to pick her up they would. Since Shaniece was older, she stayed with our neighbor until we got home – an easy arrangement because she attended school with the kids next door.

Still, we had one big challenge: distance. We lived about 45 minutes from my sister-in-law and the daunting commute— from Waldorf to DC for Raj, and Waldorf to Virginia for me – was beginning to wear on us. More than that, on the weekends we visited his family and because it was so far, we would not come back home until late evening. After three years we decided it was time to buy a home closer to them, which we did. Around this time, we also tried to have another child in accordance with the doctor's advice not to wait any more than two years. I'll spare you the details but after testing, probing, and fertility treatment, followed by my health taking another turn for the worse, it never happened. Since adoption for us was out of the question, our attitude was it was just not meant to be.

Through it all, Raj and I both continued to work, go to school, and be parents as we traded off responsibilities. Many of these years he worked two jobs and I just worked my full-time job, along with the National Guard. Yes, we were doing well but we worked for everything we had. We found ourselves wanting to get in a position where we could cut back on work hours and spend more time with each other and our kids. Most weekends I took my oldest daughter to the gym for either basketball practice or games. She played with the AAU, which dominated her entire summer and much of the school year. Eventually, our busy schedules became a little more manageable: my youngest was about three or four when I got the job with the consulting company that changed things dramatically for us years down the road. What a relief to achieve greater financial stability! Things between my *White Knight* and me could not have been better.

With respect to my newfound role in the family, I discovered life had come full-circle as I became a counselor to our teenage girls. Drawing on the example of my beloved grandmother, I coached them through a multitude of obstacles which included engaging in honest, difficult discussions about interracial issues. We were a close-knit group that shared good and bad times much, in the same way, I'd experienced as a child living with my grandparents. I enjoyed my status as a confidant and the fact that we were all there for each other. And as I'd learn, even a grown-up with children of her own occasionally needed their support as much as they needed mine.

Trouble in Paradise

One year we went on vacation with several other family members. During this trip, I dealt with unexpected events resulting in a serious conflict between Raj and me. It never occurred to me I'd ever have to handle a situation involving another woman, but from my perspective, this particular female had behaved inappropriately toward my husband by seeking him out exclusively. It was as if she needed only *his* attention. Although this put Raj and me at odds with one another in terms of how to resolve the situation, I was not the only one who'd expressed concern; another family member had also approached me about it. To my dismay, Raj seemed to dismiss my feelings on the matter and refused to confront the woman about her behavior as I'd requested.

When we returned home, the whole incident escalated out of proportion: I felt Raj was wrong for not being sensitive to my feelings and I was wrong for the way I reacted. The ensuing hurt, pain, anger, and perceived insensitivity created ever-increasing friction within our relationship over the course of several months until it inevitably erupted. I had no doubt in my mind this was the beginning of the end; I was convinced we were going to split up. Further adding to the confusion and misunderstanding were a few folks in the family who failed to comprehend what had actually transpired. In a case of excellent timing, I was scheduled to leave for deployment to Kosovo. I believed this break would prove beneficial for us in determining if we were in it for the long haul or on our way to divorce court.

Although our relationship improved dramatically prior to my departure, I still firmly believe my Kosovo deployment was the right development at the right time. In total, I spent 16 months away from home and 18 months out of the corporate environment. I came home twice: once on emergency leave and once on scheduled leave. As I discussed in an earlier chapter, during my deployment I focused on developing a healthier mental framework. I worked out two- to- three hours a day and started meditating, journaling, and thinking about what I wanted in my relationship with Raj and in my life overall.

At this point, I had completed a Master's degree and a Master's certificate program, thanks to my enrollment in the Army War

College throughout my deployment. Armed with a second Master's degree, I made partner with the consulting firm. But even though I'd achieved everything I'd set out to accomplish, I was still unhappy – mostly with myself. That monster of low self-esteem reared its ugly head again and it would take months before I got him safely under control and back into the box. I knew if I wanted to reconcile my relationship with my husband, I had to work on me, both internally and externally. This became my mission.

Raj and I talked every day I spent deployed in Kosovo. At the time we were renovating our kitchen and upgrading other rooms in our home; he would go to Home Depot and via Skype we would shop together for hours in the evenings (gotta love technology!). Funny, while many couples experience estrangement as a result of deployments, Raj and I actually grew closer. While I hated being away from my girls, it was good for him to take over the reins as both mommy and daddy while I was away. It was good for us. It put us back on track.

Upon returning home, things were wonderful and we continued to evolve as a couple. No matter how old you get, I'm not sure you ever stop growing as life takes you on an ever-changing adventure. Both of our careers were in high-gear and our daughters were thriving beyond our wildest dreams. I felt certain I'd never see another deployment because I was becoming more senior in rank – that is, until one day I was told my name was being considered for a deployment to Afghanistan.

By now I had just started an international fellows program and our youngest was about to graduate high school. Consequently, I tried to put a lid on it by advising the chief of staff I would deploy again, just not this time around. It seemed that the 29th Division picked up two rotations so I told him I would take the second. And I fulfilled my promise even though it was harder and much more emotional for me to leave this time around. My daughters and I enjoy an incredibly close bond; having to leave them with no guarantee of returning was gut-wrenching. Still, my husband and I both agreed this was a necessary step in my military career. It became a family decision, not one that was solely mine to make. My Adjutant General also agreed the deployment was necessary; being a senior leader I had to complete a combat tour. Based on my first deployment I knew Raj and I could do this.

As you might imagine, my departure was fraught with emotion, though I held my feelings inside until I reached the comforts of my room at the mob station. Prior to my leaving, Raj and I had been talking about renewing our vows for our 20-year anniversary. I felt strongly about marrying him in his faith, which meant the world to him. Because of the deployment, I told him that if and when I returned I would marry him again in a full Hindu wedding.

During the deployment, we started planning. I ordered items and worked on whatever we needed to make it successful – which turned out to be a large list. There were countless tasks that had to be completed before I got back if we stood a chance of renewing our vows close our first wedding date. Yes, *best-laid plans often go awry*. A nearly endless chain of events transpired to spoil our vision for our perfect day. While home on an early leave, I not only surprised everyone else but found myself at the receiving end of my own surprise when I found out I was being considered for General Officer. In order to position myself well for this promotion, I was required to work on a packet for submission that spring, with one of the mandatory items being a physical. It was then that the doctors expressed concern for my wellbeing and conducted additional testing and an internal sonogram of my female organs. They found a potentially cancerous growth on my ovaries and wanted to send me home immediately. I told them I needed to go back down range to wrap up transition to my deputy, and then gather my belongings. In persuading them to allow me a few weeks, I had to promise to follow their instructions to the letter. After all, what difference would a few weeks make in terms of assessment? Thankfully, they agreed. Next I had to break the news to my family by putting on the best voice I could muster. Raj and I broke down in tears, frightened of the unknown. We put the renewal plans on hold until I could get through this latest health crisis.

Needless to say, I was an emotional mess: I had to return to theater, inform my leadership, and leave my team. Even though I was only returning a month ahead of them, I felt like I was abandoning them. With the exception of losing one of our own, leaving my team behind was the hardest part of my job. And while I'm certain many others would welcome the chance to return home sooner than planned, for me it meant another few months of testing and worry.

As soon as I got back I reported to Bethesda for processing and set up appointments with specialists, including oncologists, to confront and treat my latest health scare – whatever it turned out to be. In June of that year, I was scheduled for surgery, ruining our plans to renew our vows in July because the doctors couldn't give me any guarantees regarding the extent of any potentially necessary treatment. They advised me that they would go in using small incisions and if they found signs of cancer, they would fully open me up. Of course I wasn't happy about this but had no control over the situation; there was simply no way they could determine if the mass was benign or malignant until they performed surgery. My medical team made it extremely clear that they would take the right course of action for my health either way. While hesitant and apprehensive, I knew the operation was for the best; I'd just have to remain in suspense until I woke up from the anesthesia. Only then would I discover if I had nothing to worry about or if I had to prepare myself to undergo follow-up treatment. Thankfully, I awoke to good news: I had a benign, complex cyst. Nevertheless, I still had to recover from a unilateral ovary removal but this little setback did not prevent me from reuniting with my team at the coming home ceremony.

A Storybook Wedding

During my convalescence Raj and I planned our vow renewal in preparation for a November 17 date, much closer to when we eloped. Due to our unique circumstances, we left out various aspects of the traditional Hindu marriage ceremony. For example, our nuptials would be much shorter since we were already married. And in another departure from the Hindu tradition, instead of changing three times as a bride normally would, I would only wear one outfit, in red. Still, we planned an ideal wedding any bride would dream about. Raj spent the night before at his sister's house while I hosted a Mendi party for the ladies where we indulged in henna treatments on our hands and feet. As the bride, I went first since this time-consuming ritual took a long time to dry.

We awoke early the next morning to get a jump on our full list of to-dos before the wedding, which above all involved preparing the temple. I met the delivery guy there with the sweets before approving the final touches for the ceremony. Then I returned home to shower and get my hair and makeup done. The house was buzzing with excitement leading up to our limo's arrival. From start to finish, everything was executed perfectly, much like a wedding scene from the Indian movies. First, my husband participated in special rituals that had to take place before I was brought in. I waited in a side room with my daughters, who would be the ones to cover my head, while my two sisters escorted him into the prayer area accompanied by the sounds of the Tassa drums. This traditional Indian music makes me want to dance every time I hear it.

The Tassa player indicated it was time for me to go in, prompting my daughters to cover my head in accordance with the Hindu custom. As we entered, the lighting and decorations took our breath away – the hall was adorned in golds and reds with statues of Ganesh positioned along the sides, joined by white fabric. A structure decorated with gold and yellow fabric and vibrant flowers dominated the stage, with chairs set up at the back. Off to one side, the soulful sounds of a vocalist and accompanying group provided a stirring musical backdrop. The entire scene was simply stunning. As the ceremony progressed, we arrived at the part where we each got to recite our vows. Raj had stored his on his cell phone only to forget his glasses which meant he could barely read them – go figure. To make matters worse, he also started crying. In response, the pundit remarked that the only thing he needed to do was recall his vows from memory since he was so excited to marry this woman again he couldn't even read. It was classic Raj. However, the part I anticipated most was him applying the Sindoor to my head because it showed the world I was a married woman. I was his. This meant more to me than the rest of the ceremony put together because in my mind it symbolized our unbreakable union; I was truly his in every way.

The ceremony and greetings soon ended and we headed off to the reception where I changed into a white chiffon gown, similar to what I wanted to wear when we married the first time. Once again our reception colors were royal blue and white. The Tassa players led us into the celebration and upon arriving at the center of the floor, we danced to the Tassa before ending with our first dance. Looking into each other's eyes as we moved to the music, I knew without a doubt we were made for each other; it also warmed my heart to realize just how elated Raj had been with the day's festivities. Other highlights of the evening were the classical Indian dance of Rama and Seeta performed beautifully and gracefully by our youngest daughter, and a toast led by our oldest. In the end, the reception turned out just as magnificently as the ceremony. But wouldn't you know it, the night ended with Raj again passed out.

Over multiple decades, we have grown together as a couple. Raj has been my partner, my friend, and my confidant during these years; never once did he ever tell me I could not do or be something. Instead, he has supported me through every venture I took on.

When people ask how I did it, I find it difficult to explain other than saying it was hard work. But when you have someone who believes in you when you don't believe in yourself, someone who is there to take the poundings when you don't know where to place the blame – that's when you know you have met your soulmate. It goes far beyond honoring the vows for better or for worse; it entails loving each other unconditionally.

A Reason, A Season, A Lifetime

Throughout my life, many people have crossed my path. These individuals were clients, peers, subordinates, supervisors, coaches, mentors and sponsors in addition to family and friends. It is crucial to recognize and understand the importance of having these types of relationships at varying points in your life. Career-wise, the relationships you form and the networks you build are essential to your success; they will carry you through the most challenging times. Often, you will learn from these individuals in ways you never imagined, bringing a whole new meaning to perpetual learning.

My ongoing education never stopped yet I was always amazed at how much I still did not know. The relationships I formed at the company and in the military were one of the main reasons I stayed – I thrived on the connection with a broader group of like-minded people who were on a mission to enact positive change in their own way. Whether a senior level commander, coordinating staff, general officer, account lead, defense lead, government lead, operating unit lead, or even operations officer, I found people who believed in me more than I believed in myself at times. They showed me I could be more and was capable of doing more. Having worked for both female and male leaders, I can truly say there was no difference in capability. Yes, there are always differences in people but they were all highly capable and many of them were excellent leaders.

I have discovered if you open yourself up you will be surprised by how much you can learn from others simply by being in their presence. When you work around truly talented and skilled people, your outlook extends beyond the horizon. Conversely, you can learn the most from those who work for you; it's simply amazing what you can discover when you allow yourself to listen to what they say. I know that if not for these relationships, I would not be successful.

All of the countless hours of my life during which I've been coached and mentored I have repaid in countless hours spent coaching and mentoring others. It is only fair that we pay it forward by helping our fellow human beings. Through the act of paying it forward, I found my true self. It never occurred to me until the last five or so years that I am happiest when I am doing unto others just as they have done to me – so many times I've actually lost count. Being able to see beyond your blind spots requires you to open all of your senses in order to take in all that surrounds you, and this can only happen after you've reached your own level of self-awareness. It is through others that we learn more about ourselves. These are the experiences we should seek out in order to be better human beings today than we were yesterday. Don't underestimate the power of the relationships you form, whether personal or professional. Sometimes the two will intertwine. I truly do believe that every individual comes in and out of our lives purposefully; therefore, we should be just as deliberate with our intentions and actions. It is now abundantly clear to me that the relationships I've formed over my 50-plus years on earth have served a higher purpose: to assist in my path toward finding me.

CHAPTER 8

SEPARATION ANXIETY – HOW CAN I HELP YOU SAY GOODBYE?

I often ask myself the question, *when is being gone too much?* As with most difficult life choices, the answer is unique to every individual. In my case, I have always traveled for work, often away for several weeks at a time or on the road Monday through Friday, returning home on weekends. This hectic travel schedule was the norm in my civilian job though I was fortunate I didn't have to pick up and leave week after week and year after year like some of my peers. While I did manage a few out-of-town projects, the majority of them were local, which meant I only had to board a plane or take a road trip about once or twice per month.

Growing up, separation from loved ones was not an understood concept because my family didn't travel. I didn't have to cope with people coming and going. I'm not even certain if my grandparents ever traveled more than a few hours away from home or if they ever flew somewhere on a plane. Although nowadays flying is as common as driving and long commutes to work are generally accepted, I still believe most of us cannot imagine what it's like to be separated from our families for extended periods of time – whether for several months or more than a year.

In the military, of course, separation is the norm. The sacrifices men and women in uniform make extend far beyond the complex environments in which they operate. Rarely do civilians see the havoc that takes place in their personal lives as we ask them to serve their country, yet in spite of the hardship they perform their duties well and don't ask for much in return. But Americans should, at least, recognize that their honor and commitment to the United States comes at a cost that we as a society can never repay. We can never do enough to compensate for their losses. The best we can do is provide recognition and support to our service members and their families for their ongoing sacrifices so that we may continue to live in the land of the free.

A Revolving Door of Absentee Parents

As a young child, I never understood why I didn't live with my parents. Yes, I loved and adored my grandparents who took excellent care of me but try explaining to a little girl why her mother and father only come around to visit once in a while. I'd constantly have thoughts like, *why do you leave me each time, why do you take my brother and sister but not me?* The entire arrangement made me question whether or not they were really my parents and why they didn't want me. The happiest time in my childhood was when I lived in my grandparents' home where I was loved, cherished, and respected. Yet it still didn't help me to understand my estranged relationship with the people who gave me life; my reaction to their visits was typical for a child who was trying to make sense of her world. The moment they arrived, I loved to climb onto my mother's lap; in those days she actually allowed it. Occasionally, she'd even lavish me with kisses. At that age, all I wanted was to be close to her. My mother's beauty awed and inspired me.

She would walk through the door wearing a flared, pretty dress with her hair piled in a bun on top of her head while my dad always sported dress slacks or some type of nice, casual attire. Sometimes they would play softball with us down the hill in a small area we'd use for that purpose. The best part for me was standing in the outfield surrounded by apple trees, not actively paying attention. Believe it or not, my mother could really play. My dad had a blast striking everyone out with his famous fastball. Once, my mom slipped and fell as she was running to the base, resulting in a hugely swollen knee. After that, I'm not sure how much she participated in our games.

However, no matter how much fun we'd have together, I'd run and hide when it was time for them to leave because I believed if they couldn't find me to say goodbye, they wouldn't go. Sometimes I'd cry and beg them to take me with them, and they'd assure me they would after their next visit. But when they came back again, I still couldn't go home with them. It was just too much for my young mind to accept or comprehend. I didn't see them every weekend but the pattern invariably remained the same: I'd either hide, or cry and beg when they left, and they'd offer an empty promise of taking me with them the "next time." As for the emotional fallout of their departure, Mom-mom and Aunt Sissie had to deal with my broken heart and help me pick up the pieces. Sometimes my grandfather would take me for a ride to the general store where I would get candy or a soda pop – anything to take my mind off of it.

Still, it wasn't all bad. During the holidays, especially Christmas, they would bring all kinds of gifts for us. The guys usually got tools and while I don't remember what the girls received, I would get a new outfit or a Barbie doll. Most importantly, my parents never failed to bring a gift for everyone during these years.

So Close and Yet So Far

As I mentioned before, I moved in with my parents on my ninth birthday. Without a doubt, this was an intensely emotional time for many of my family members, not just me. While it seemed cool to want to live with them in a new house, it was harder than you can imagine. Even now, I remember many events from that day in detail as if they were permanently etched in my mind. What should have been one of the happiest moments of my life was marred by a multitude of factors. First, it felt like a sneak attack on my grandparents, who were not home that day and thus denied the courtesy of saying goodbye.

My parents had been on the land, waiting to put the finishing touches on their section home. An amazing sight to see, it had been delivered in two sections and came fully furnished. Once it was operational, they came for me with the promise of a birthday cake and celebration. As a child I had no idea what I was agreeing to, enamored by their enticements and assurance I could visit my grandparents anytime I wanted. What I was not expecting was the torment and abuse that would characterize the remainder of my childhood and adolescence in the days, weeks, months, and years to follow.

In a sign of events to come, my mother rummaged through my clothes and decided what I could and could not keep. I had a little blue trunk filled with items I treasured including my paper dolls, notebooks in which I wrote stories, my records, and some other prized possessions. Unmoved by how much I cherished these personal belongings, my mother forbade me to bring them to my new home. Whatever she did allow me to keep was first subject to inspection for several days, due to her fear of roaches. Despite my second thoughts about moving in with my parents, it was a done deal. I cried myself to sleep for several nights, longing to go back to my grandparents' loving, safe environment. It seemed this was definitely not an option.

While my parents may have had good intentions, their execution left much to be desired. I hate to sound unappreciative but as a young girl, this was a monumental adjustment. Looking back on the experience makes me appreciate what children go through when abandoned by their parents. At least, I had wonderful grandparents who loved and treated me as their own during the early part of my life. That foundation sustained me through the rough times though the shadow of doubt as to why I was the one my parents gave away haunted me for years. I experienced a range of emotions as a result of my upbringing, a natural consequence my parents never took into consideration. *Did they even think about the longer-term effects and how words and actions really mean something?*

For example, I fielded all sorts of questions about my brother and sister from the kids at school who didn't believe we were related and thought I was lying. I would have to explain as best as I could – a challenge for a kid who didn't fully understand the circumstances herself. Conversely, it was nearly impossible for my classmates to comprehend. Sometimes I just wanted things to go back to the way they were. While I did not develop any emotional or mental problems like anxiety and panic disorder or depression, there were inexplicable things going on inside of me, things I couldn't understand. If I were to ask my siblings today, most likely they'd remark that I should have just accepted the change because it was not a big deal. But the difference lies in our divergent experiences: they came from an opposite frame of reference; what constituted a major upheaval for me was nothing more than a change of address for them.

This is a truism of life. We all filter events through our unique prisms and perspectives, based on our origins and upbringing. While children don't initially understand the concept of biases – they learn them by the words and actions of the adults around them – we should teach them what it means to understand, demonstrate compassion, and respect the differences in others including the way they look and think, and their innate capabilities.

With the benefit of hindsight and maturity, I've discovered that fate sometimes has other plans for us. As an adult, I can reason through the most horrific events of my life but as a child I didn't have a sophisticated level of thinking, nor did I possess the experience to apply logic to them in order to make peace within myself. I will admit, things do have a way of working out because maybe, just maybe, God knows best. In my later years I dealt with separation from the majority of my family when I left home but this time, it was significantly different in the sense that I was angry. I felt as if I had the wind knocked out of me. Here I thought I was doing the right thing by telling my parents what my brother did to me; how he violated and abused me. It never crossed my mind that I would be ordered to leave home. I was achieving academically and athletically in school and laying out the foundation for my career as I started focusing on what I wanted to do after graduation.

When my circumstances totally shifted because of this incident, I forgot about all of my plans and goals for my life and went into survival mode. Even now as an accomplished grown-up I still remember what I was doing that fateful day – cooking fried chicken for dinner. Back then, our house had an "open concept" design with the family room, kitchen, and dining area set up in various spaces of one expansive room. My parents were sitting on the couch drinking as I prepared the food. I don't remember exactly how the conversation went down – just that it ended with Mom hurling vicious, vulgar insults at me.

As you might imagine, in a perfect combination of both of my parents I had quite a temper. When the aspersions began to fly, I did my best to ignore them until my mother started accusing me of encouraging the rape. It was at that moment I felt I had to stand up for myself by talking back. When she got up as if threatening me with bodily harm, my dad intervened; however, subduing her rage was easier said than done. I just made matters worse by going at her in kind. There we were, with Dad in the middle and Mom screaming she was going to kill me and to shut my mouth because this was her house. When my father advised me to leave, it struck me to the core. *I did not cause this. This was not my fault so why am I the one who has to leave?* I was hurt, angry, and frankly just pissed off about the whole situation.

Motherhood, Guilt, and Responsibility

When I had my first baby Shaniece, staying at home was not an option. Once she was four or five weeks old, I had to secure child care as much as I hated the idea of leaving her to go to work. Once in a while, my sister would watch her, but most of the time she had to work too. I faced tremendous anxiety putting Shaniece in the care of strangers; if I'd had a choice, I definitely would have made a different decision. Ultimately I found a local daycare provider, someone referred to me by one of my neighbors. Because she was a military spouse for whom I received good references, I thought I'd done a fairly good job reviewing her background. At first, things seemed to go well...that is until Shaniece developed diaper rash not long after she started going there.

I spoke to the daycare provider about it and asked her to make sure my baby was being changed appropriately. Throughout the day, I'd call to check on Shaniece and most of the time the provider wouldn't answer the phone – a definite cause for concern. One day my sister offered to pick the baby up early and became suspicious when the daycare provider didn't answer the door. When she heard kids crying, she became even more alarmed and decided to look into her patio door and knock from there. She spotted the provider's three-year-old son and the other kids but could not see her. My sister waited a while, then finally saw the provider approaching from the direction of the shopping center, which meant that she had left other people's babies and toddlers alone with her three-year-old son. That's right: my four-month-old had been left unattended.

According to my sister, who immediately called me at work to tell me what happened, Shaniece's diaper was soaked through and she was crying up a storm. Later that evening, I called the provider to inform her I would not be bringing my baby back, nor would I be paying her for that day. Astoundingly, the next morning she showed up at my apartment. I'd just finished feeding Shaniece and was still in my robe when she confronted me about what had happened. I reiterated that I was still not going to pay her for that day due to her negligence. I also advised her of my plan to call the police if I found out that she did this again with other children. To my surprise, she spat in my face and took off running.

Not thinking, I went after her in my robe with no shoes on my feet in spite of the cold temperatures outside. When the door slammed behind me I totally lost it, knowing I was now locked out; I was never so scared in my life. While I didn't panic, I was frantic and ran straight to the security office in the next building so they could let me in. That daycare provider is lucky I realized what happened and stopped pursuing her because my focus shifted back to my child. Later, I reported her to social services to ensure that someone looked into her practices. As for daycare, my neighbor and supervisor at the restaurant where I was working part-time agreed to watch her during my shift. She would stay at home until I returned or bring her to the restaurant where we would swap. In a pinch, she came through for me.

Luckily after that, I did not have to get a daycare provider for Shaniece again until she was about two-and-a-half years old. By then, I'd left my ex to move back to the DC area permanently and felt overly anxious about being away from my child. I still hated to leave but spent quality time with her when we were together. Because of the initial incident with daycare, I learned to apply much more diligence when researching providers. What a relief it was when she started school and I could enroll her in before and after care.

The biggest challenge with being a single parent is that you don't have the option of staying at home with your child every single day; therefore, making the most of the time you do spend together becomes even more important. Yet when you work around the clock to make ends meet and keep food on the table, it's extremely difficult to guarantee quality in every parent-child interaction. I was blessed with Shaniece who was a good baby; even when she grew into a little girl, she never fussed when it was time for me to go. It bothered me to be away from her so much, but I knew if I didn't work, I couldn't take care of her. If I wanted to give her a better life, I had no choice but to earn a living and advance my career. Thankfully, our time spent apart did not have a detrimental effect on her and she matured into a fine young woman.

Eleven years later, it felt like déjà vu as I found myself having to leave my second daughter, Tara to go back to work. I relived all of the emotional upheaval – the anxiety, the self-recriminations, the belief I was a bad parent – you name it. Leaving her to go to the office every day was difficult; I missed her terribly as I went about my business. However, knowing she was in the capable, loving hands of my sister-in-law made a huge difference this time around. Not only would she be properly cared for, she'd probably be a little spoiled too.

However, we faced a new challenge as she got older – her attachment to Raj. Tara came down with a cold when she was about five or six months old, which exacerbated her colic and sleeping problems. My efforts to soothe her back to sleep failed so Raj and I took turns comforting her until finally he brought her into our room, where he laid on the bed with her. When he placed her against his chest, she finally succumbed. This went on for several nights; we had no idea it would create a huge issue in such a short amount of time.

Tara got so attached to him she didn't want him out of her sight. It got so bad that Raj would walk around the house with her strapped to his chest in a carrier because she had to be wherever he was. You would have thought he was the mom the way she would cling to him. Whenever he had to leave for work I would have to take her upstairs to play until he was gone; once she realized her daddy was nowhere to be found she'd throw a tantrum. To say she didn't like to be separated from him would be an understatement. As a matter of fact, when she got older and learned how to tell time, we had to inform her exactly what time we would pick her up from her aunt's house or from daycare. If we were late, Tara clearly expressed her displeasure.

When I think about my separation anxiety with my own kids, I often wonder if my parents felt the same way every time they left me. Did they truly miss me? Even though my husband and I both worked, our daughters are especially close to us even to this day. If I'm out of town, they'll call me. If our schedules get hectic, they check in to see if I'm doing alright. We schedule dinner dates at least once a week and plan mother-daughter outings when we can sync calendars. Even though they are in their 20's and 30's, Tara and Shaniece will always be my babies.

Dealing with Deployments and Thoughts Left Unspoken

Most might view separation anxiety as something that only occurs when you are small but it affects people at every age. After spending a significant amount of time in the Reserves and National Guard, it was clear in early 2000 that our world as we knew it was changing. I had friends and soldiers being deployed left and right. Just when we thought things would slow down, September 11, 2001, happened. Before I knew it, I found myself standing in front of one of my units telling them it would be ok as I sent them off to battle with my apologies for not being able to accompany them.

While I shipped off many of my troops, it wasn't until December of 2005 that I received an email to call one of my staff officers. His message took me by surprise though I cannot recall exactly what ran through my mind. I was about five minutes from my civilian employer and had an executive breakfast to attend in less than 20 minutes. Once I got to the office I called to see what the issue was all about; much to my astonishment, my staff officer shared his theory that I was being considered to deploy with the 29th Division. He then informed me the chief of staff was waiting for my call. Well as it turned out, his intuition was correct: the chief of staff told me I was being deployed as the Division Chief of Staff for Logistics. He further apprised me I would be transferred to the division and begin drilling with them in January of 2006 for initial planning, training, and preparation.

All of this occurred before 7:30 in the morning and by the time I got to the executive breakfast I was reeling with emotions. What had just happened hit me out of the blue, igniting a reverberation of countless, conflicting thoughts through my mind. I tried to be my usual jovial self, but couldn't figure out how to remove the "scared shitless" expression from my face. Having already lost a soldier to war during the time I was deploying units within my battalion to Iraq, I knew there was great risk involved, along with plenty of uncertainty. The only silver lining was that I was being deployed to Kosovo instead of Iraq but even that couldn't quell the eruption of conflicted feelings.

I looked around the room at my co-workers and friends, realizing I was going to have to leave them for some unspecified period. Simultaneously, I was concerned for my burgeoning career: without a doubt, my deployment would put a halt to my steady climb up the corporate ladder, at least for the duration of my absence. But the hardest part was yet to come. In my mind I fast-forwarded to the day I had to get on the plane, imagining a heart-wrenching goodbye. Ultimately my family handled it well and together we got through it.

The anxiety and guilt you experience at the mere thought of leaving your loved ones is just as bad as actually leaving them.

These emotions tend to tag-team and wear on you for the duration. If you're not careful, they can utterly debilitate you. It's tough to console your kids when you feel the same fear, apprehension, and sadness they do. In the end, I was gone for 16 months during my first deployment but it went better than expected and we were able to put it behind us. Still, leaving never gets easier. At my going away party, I remember crying with several of my family members, none of us daring to articulate the question on everyone's mind: *Was it my destiny to return?* It's the toughest aspect of deployment for all soldiers: there is no guarantee you'll make it home alive. We all know it but we don't talk about it.

Fast forwarding again to 2011, we had been at war for more than a decade and as many of us know, you should never get complacent in wartime. Instinctively I knew if things continued on the same course, the potential for another deployment was likely. In fact, it was inevitable; it was just a matter of time before I got the notification. Prior to my official notice, I'd been hearing rumors that my name was on the list for deployment to Afghanistan. Proactively I began to prepare my family, which meant engaging in several discussions pertaining to my impending deployment. Through it all, my husband remained a stalwart champ who helped me realize that this was exactly what I was trained to do. Although older, my daughters were not as happy.

My youngest took it the hardest; if it had been up to her someone else would have gone in my place. Raj and I felt confident that this deployment would be a breeze based on how well we handled the first one. Well, don't let anyone fool you: leaving your family for a deployment *never* gets easier and the accompanying anxiety and apprehension never go away. I thought I could deal with it but felt as if I'd lost a big part of me. I'm sure many of you can relate to that feeling of being punched in the gut and having the air knocked right out of you. Whether caused by a military deployment, health crisis, death, or some other tragic event, the ensuing emotional turmoil can be devastating.

However, nothing is worse than realizing your family is suffering in the same way and there's nothing you can do but attempt to console them. You realize you have to be the strong one for their sake. This second deployment took a toll on my family that was almost too much for them to handle. They all worried about my safety but my youngest developed a separation anxiety that was far more difficult to deal with than you can imagine. Every time she went past my vehicle in the garage it seemed to trigger a panic or anxiety attack. I realized her emotions were similar to the ones I experienced when my parents removed me from my grandparents' home. While anxiety did not consume me, just remembering how conflicted I was back then compelled me to reassure her as much as I could. It didn't help that she was in her first year of college which is always a big transition for young people. Combined with the reality of the dangers of the daily circumstances unfolding in Afghanistan, often sensationalized in the media, it was a rough time for my youngest daughter. Although I successfully appealed to our state Chaplain to talk with her, I worried she might begin using medicine to control her anxiety and panic disorder – an outcome I definitely didn't want. Based on our example of surviving the previous deployment, I felt confident we could survive this one. And by the grace of God, we did.

Be an Overcomer

Separation anxiety is real. Even though we may dismiss our symptoms or attribute them to something else entirely doesn't mean we're not experiencing them. The key is to become cognizant of these feelings and learn to manage them, rather than allowing them to consume or paralyze us. I am sure if you ask my youngest, she will tell you her anxiety debilitated her to the point where she could barely function, if at all, on some days. As a parent, it was my job to help her develop coping skills to navigate her way through. Thanks to my last deployment, Tara still has to work on managing her anxiety, along with depression.

The good news? I can tell you with absolute certainty there are a multitude of non-prescription alternatives available to help you work through the problem. But that does not mean everyone has the ability to manage it well on their own. If you need to seek out medical attention or counseling, do so. In my case, I developed some effective coping methods which included finding that safe place within myself where I could find some sort of peace. How did I get to there? I would listen to uplifting music every day when I got back to my room. It was a ritual I engaged in during my first deployment and it always reminded me of the good things back home.

No matter how you deal with anxiety, depending on how much energy you can muster you may have to take it one moment, one hour, or one day at a time. Notwithstanding my coping skills, I had my moments of emotional weakness. For example, I always enjoyed my phone calls with the family back home, but during the holidays they were tough. We'd invariably dissolve into tears before the end of the conversation, knowing how much I love the Christmas season, my favorite time of the year.

Channeling the anxiety and adjusting your perspective are crucial; you must avoid falling into the trap of believing your current state of mind is a permanent condition. Sometimes the memories may be too overwhelming, but talking about how much you miss your loved ones and how wonderful they are will fill you with immense pride. As for our children, they are much more resilient than we think. We owe it to them to ensure they have the best care possible, whether we are with them or not. While separation is hard, I do believe it makes the heart grow fonder and inspires us to treasure the things we think we've lost. But most importantly, it makes us appreciate our loved ones' little quirks and idiosyncracies – along with their frustrating qualities – when we happily to return to their loving arms.

CHAPTER 9
EFFECTIVE COMMUNICATION: LISTENING WITH INTENT, SPEAKING WITH CLARITY

Communication is an important activity many of us do not engage in as well as we should. When I think back over my career, I realize there have been times when my communication was effective and times when it left much to be desired. In my years of experience, I have discovered that communication entails more than what is said. In fact, what is left unsaid potentially holds even greater power and often causes hurt feelings and misunderstandings.

In many of my life experiences I've discussed thus far, you could say that my major failures and successes hinged upon communication – whether competent or ineffective. It's ironic that communication plays such a vital role in all aspects of our lives yet we spend so little time cultivating and improving the manner in which we listen, comprehend, and speak. As a leader, I am committed to spending time developing my communication skills to ensure understanding among all parties and points of view. I applied the principles I learned to every facet of my life; whether at home, in the office, or even in a public place like a restaurant. In all of my interactions I have attempted to be as clear as possible, knowing we are often judged by our style of communication and our ability to express ourselves well. Because it makes an impact on every relationship and situation we experience, I firmly believe that all individuals should make an ongoing effort to develop and improve their communication skills.

Cultural Intricacies and the Language of Friendship

From kindergarten to fifth grade, my youngest daughter Tara was in a French immersion program. The teachers immersed her and her classmates in the French language from day one, even though many of them had no clue what was being said, nor did their parents. So can you imagine what it was like to have a young child who could read and write in French but had problems processing the English concepts. We knew she was learning based on the homework; however, helping her make the leap in concepts over to English presented a problem. Typically, when I helped her with her assignments, I would have to spend time translating to understand what she was being asked to do – a task that was much easier when it came to reading but much harder when it involved math.

We soon discovered we only needed to speak her language in terms of interests to help make the connection between the French and English sentence structure. Tara could read a book in French with no issues but if you gave her a book in English, she struggled. Eventually, we found a short program that focused on teaching children phonetics by making it fun for them to learn the concepts. Most importantly, the program taught us as parents the importance of appealing to her interests to entice her to read more. After thinking the matter over, we realized we could tap into her enjoyment of Pokemon, which also had a series of books we could purchase. We made the trip to the bookstore a big deal and bought her several of the first books in the series. While I could not even pronounce half of the names in the book, Tara got it. After reading every book in the series, she became an avid reader from that point forward. Finding her language was more about discovering something that piqued her interest, which helped to bridge the gap between the concepts that had previously eluded her. Our daughter then developed a healthy addiction to books: for about six years, that was all she wanted for Christmas – whether wrapped and waiting for her under the tree or picked out during a visit to the bookstore. I had never before witnessed a child at seven or eight who could spend literally two-hundred dollars in a bookstore on Anime books. What started out as a struggle turned into an obsession. To this day, Tara loves to read and will not sacrifice having a hard copy of a book in her hands.

When she was sixteen, I spent some time in Boston with a business colleague who was from France. He had three sons and his youngest was the same age as Tara. After talking it over at length, we made an agreement to see if our kids might have an interest in taking turns staying with each other's families in their respective countries. As an initial step, we put the two kids in touch with one another via Skype. Soon after, they mutually decided that Matthew would come from France first so he could practice English and see the US; this would also help Tara practice her French. Although it turned out to be a great visit, when I first saw this blond-haired, blue-eyed young man get off the plane, I asked myself what I'd done. While the young girls in the family immediately flipped over him, Tara was a much harder sell. It took a tremendous effort to get her to interact with him and several days before they warmed up to each other in spite of the countless hours they'd spent communicating over the computer. The overall visit went well but Tara opted not to go to stay with Matthew's family in France. However, we did end up taking a vacation there and met up with all of them during our visit to Paris. Even better, Tara acted as our interpreter, which made the trip more enjoyable since I had only studied the language for a semester in high school and did not possess a deep level of conversational French. Once she reached the fifth grade, Tara did not want to stay in the French immersion program. Instead, she took Japanese, a language she was trying to learn all by herself. In my estimation, Anime greatly influenced her interest in the Japanese language and culture.

With Tara in the Japanese program in high school, we decided it would be a great experience to host an exchange student. While this comes with great excitement, when children get attached to you and you to them, it is hard to say goodbye. What I loved most was just getting to know each and every one of our special guests. It made for interesting interactions because I hardly knew any of the language. One particular incident stands out in my mind. I remember showing our exchange student to the guest room upon her arrival to our home. After she had packed away her things, she came to the top of the rear stairs to ask if she could use the wash machine. Although a bit confused I said yes, knowing that she'd been in the states for at least a week; if washing clothes was a priority for her, I would gladly help. But when I explained my willingness to assist, she looked at me with a confused expression on her face. I reiterated that if she brought me her dirty laundry, I would wash her clothes for her. Observing her obvious puzzlement, I realized something was not making sense, so I asked Tara to translate. When they both started laughing, I knew that something had gone astray. Turned out, she just wanted to use the shower and wondered why I'd offer to help her with that! This amusing story illustrates the power of words and the fact that the simplest of things can cause misunderstandings.

Trini Linguistics

Another challenge I had to face early on in my relationship with Raj was understanding the Trini's. While someone from Trinidad speaks English, the accent, local dialect, and words used to express various concepts combine to create a completely different language. In the beginning, I had a hard time following the conversation and would sometimes get a headache from trying so hard. Sometimes, I would give the pretense of comprehending simply by smiling and nodding in certain places. When you are listening to people talk and hear things like "gih mih de flickin ting nah" or "yur dotish," which I now understand to be "give me the damn thing please" or "you're stupid," it makes you wonder if that wine you were drinking went to your head with the first sip. Sometimes my sister-in-law would say "ay com lime nah" which means "are you coming to hang out?" Dating Raj meant having to learn a completely new language intermingled with English.

The communication differences even affected things like Trini music, when songs would refer to "whining." Far from the concept most of us think of, in the Trini sense, "whining" is about gyrating your hips. Early on in my relationship with Raj, I remember having a conversation with my brother-in-law as we were all sitting around and talking. He asked Raj, "Is that your doolahin?" prompting me to look at him as if he had lost his ever loving mind. I had no clue what he meant and did not even know how to spell it to begin to try to understand. Knowing I was completely stumped, they all broke out in laughter. I accused them of having fun at my expense and asked them to explain what he meant. My brother-in-law chuckled and informed me that he wanted to know if I was Raj's bride. This conversation took place well before we got married, so from that point on, they would frequently refer to me as his doolahin as a running joke.

One day my sister-in-law and some other family members were cooking in my kitchen and started asking me for things, one of them being bhandanya. I looked at her with confusion and asked, "what is that?" She cracked up as she tried to explain that it is essentially a green herb plant that they grind up to make seasoning for meat. Little-by-little I began to understand Trini slang to the point where I don't even have to think about the conversation anymore. Conversely, however, this presents another challenge in that it is easy for some of the terminology to creep into my everyday language, which, in a business environment, may cause a problem. For many reasons, I had to learn to turn it on and off. Still, there were times it would sneak into my conversation like on the day I went to a sub shop for lunch with several co-workers. When the guy behind the counter asked me what I wanted to drink, I responded with "what kind of sweetdrink do ya have?" He looked at me and asked, "where are you from?" When I informed him I was from Maryland, he didn't believe me because the only people he knew who referred to soda as "sweetdrink" are from the islands. I just started to laugh when I realized what he meant. It had rolled off my tongue so naturally, I hadn't even thought about it.

But my immersion in Trini slang goes even deeper since Tara spent a significant amount of time around my in-laws. Once she could talk, she sounded like a Trini. One day when she was playing in our closet and the tack strip stuck her finger, she came to us and announced, "something jook me na." Raj and I looked at each other and fought to contain our laughter to prevent her from getting mad. But when you spend so much time with family, it's tough to avoid having things rub off on you. In fact, I worked hard to understand not only the language but their culture. It intrigued me so much, I just enjoyed the process of discovering their unique customs and distinctive approach to life in general.

My brother in law, Blacks, and his brother, Mocho would constantly tease me when we were together. They were talking one day and assumed I didn't understand them. Mocho addressed me as "ay Linz" (he never seemed to call me Linda), "wine na" and I jumped up and started wining my waist and singing the song. He then said to Blacks, "oh god she know" and started laughing. We often indulged in this kind of light-hearted bantering; while an outsider who didn't know us would have thought they were laughing at me, in reality, they were laughing just to have fun which made it fun for everyone else. What I can honestly tell you is that learning and appreciating the language disparities as well as the culture expanded my lens significantly. I formed a greater appreciation for the differences we all bring to the table and how being able to listen – truly listen to what is being said and/or what is *not* being said, is absolutely critical. Many of us make assumptions based on misperceptions. In this particular case, I could have easily taken offense to their actions when they were simply trying to make me feel like I was part of the family.

On the other hand, learning the Trini language has it pluses and minuses. When Tara was about two years old, she loved to play with her Uncle Blacks to the point where she would mimic everything he did. One day he was teasing her as per his usual routine; she would grab onto his bald head and they would make all kinds of noise. I don't know what happened or whether or not she got mad at him or was truly copying him but kids tend to pick up all kinds of habits or words you'd rather they didn't. While Tara and Uncle Blacks were playing this game in which he would grab her arm and start running his fingers down it to her armpit, she always laughed and begged him to do it over and over again. But for some reason on this particular occasion, she had no interest in playing with him which she expressed by hitting him. Although he moved out of the way she then called him a "mother ass," somewhat under her breath, but loud enough for us to think that is what we heard. He asked, "what did you call me?" and she just put her head down and refused to speak. She'd uttered this expression, at least, one other time we could recall; we then had to make a decision as to how to proceed. If we made a big deal out of it, would she stop? Or was it better to ignore it altogether? Based on the way she acted, we made the decision to let it go. It turned out to be the right course of action because eventually she stopped saying it. We found that reprimanding her only caused her to repeat the behavior we wanted to change. Funny, life has a way of coming full circle; evidently Raj constantly got punished for cussing up a storm when he was young. Truly the apple does not fall far from the tree.

Uniform Confusion

It's endlessly amusing how the simplest tasks can get jumbled up thanks to language nuances, mixed messages, and communication in general. Sometimes, no matter how hard you try, things still can get misconstrued. When I was in officer candidate school, a situation arose that got blown way out of proportion. We reported on a Friday evening and stayed through late afternoon on Sunday and for whatever reason, this one weekend in particular just started out in a stressful manner. Upon reporting, we were told that there would be a uniform inspection. Since we weren't sure which uniform was required, the guys were supposed to let us know; because of the duty positions, they'd receive the communication first. Between drill and upon showing up, we'd received so much conflicting information, I realized I did not have all of my dress uniform. We tried to rectify the communication issue between the males and females using walkie-talkies but even the most well thought out plan can have flaws if you don't think things through. They were having a hard time communicating the uniform but the one I needed was a full Class A. It just so happened someone else was missing something for theirs while I was just missing the pants. Therefore, we tried to find out if anyone else had extra pants that would fit and figure out a way to make up for other missing parts. Unfortunately, we had no workable solution to the problem and would not know which uniform would be inspected until morning. So we got this bright idea that after lights-out, we would send two people, keeping the buddy concept, to get additional pants. We also decided that we could only be gone for a short period which meant having to go to the closest female's house. Since I lived almost 75 miles away, my place was definitely not an option.

Although we successfully executed our plan, we did not take into account the difference in height between all of us. When the morning came and the males communicated to us, we started out in our battle dress uniform for inspection. As per their standard procedure, the TACs waited until we got into formation to inform us we needed to change because we were wearing the wrong one. Since we'd been in a different location than the males, both communication and distance presented an issue with receiving the proper instruction. Although they had been aware of the uniform change, they neglected to share the information with the females in time. Consequently, we showed up in battle dress and the males in dress uniform. Where is the fairness in that? All they had to offer was a lame, "Sorry we didn't notify you guys," and we all got into trouble. The TACs gave us roughly ten minutes to be back in formation changed in full dress uniform for inspection. Just what I was dreading: Class A inspection.

In order to make it work, at least, four of us switched pants in the end. While we made it to formation within the allotted time, I was sweating bullets and had no clue what was going to transpire when they came down the line to do the inspection. When the TAC officers got to me and looked me up and down, they could barely keep a straight face. Let me just explain why. While my pants mostly fit, they were about four inches too short, which made me look hideous. As we tried to keep straight faces, the situation proved too comical; only the fear of getting into even more trouble helped us contain our laughter. Now as one of the candidates who always seemed to have her stuff together, this was way out of the ordinary for me. But I suppressed my desire to crack up for the good of my team.

As a result of this experience, we learned that no matter how much you try to communicate clearly, there is always the potential for something to go awry. The real test is how you deal with the fallout. Sure, we could have blamed the guys but that approach would have only gotten us into more trouble and missed the overall point. Our position, or more specifically, my position, was that it took teamwork for us to make this work; if that meant switching clothes, then we were there for one another, regardless of the breakdown in communication. Ultimately, the TAC officers decided to dig a little deeper in order to understand how many of us had to switch clothes to make the uniform situation somewhat right. Out of eight females, half of us switched all during a ten-minute limit. What's the lesson here? Make sure you clarify, check, and double check when everything relies on messages getting to the right level and to all personnel. Sometimes no matter what you do, you can't defeat the inevitable even with the best communication methods. While I lived through the incident, I will never forget it. And it all started with a minor communication flaw. Isn't that how all issues of this nature start?

Undertones: Reading Between the Lines

Workplace communication is vastly different in that there can be many more factors at play than what we experience in school, at home, or outside of the office. The dynamics of the professional environment can be daunting; throw in communication mishaps and it can be a recipe for disaster. While the understanding of body language, facial expressions, eye movement, and many other facets that underscore communication is crucial, these are also the elements that are talked about at great length. What amazes me is what is *not* normally discussed, or expressed as lessons learned, the things we tend to gloss over or avoid addressing altogether. Two immediately come to mind. The first is passive behavior, which is a natural result of what is not being said by an individual's actions. Often, passive behavior is based on the biases we form from our own experiences; we bring these biases into everything we do and if we fail to comprehend how it impacts the situation, then things can really get out of hand. Regardless of the work situation, passive behavior can and does occur in all of them. It first starts off as someone being more comfortable with one person or, if they are not as familiar with an individual with whom they are partnering with for a specific purpose, they make assumptions about them. In my experience, I've discovered that in many cases if someone has a perception about me, that perception becomes the reality I'm forced to address and overcome.

Throughout my career, there have been times when I've collaborated on proposals with teams of individuals. In the beginning, they would assign everyone a specific role to support the proposal process. In one case, I was doing research and writing, and helping to pull together multiple parts of the proposal. Throughout the process, we held meetings to discuss various technical or functional approaches. Most of the time I remained fairly quiet unless I felt a need to discuss a topic that no one else had mentioned. During some of the meetings, many people talked over each other in their zeal to make their points; they just could not wait until someone seemed as if they were going to stop speaking before they would jump in. This usually drove me crazy because I always felt like they were trying to show off just how smart they were. Maybe it was their way of contributing but from my foxhole, it prolonged the meetings unnecessarily. I'd watch, listen, and focus on whoever was speaking to gather what I needed to take away from the conversation in order to improve my part of the proposal.

Typically, a few nuggets would surface. The executive leading the effort made some assumptions based on his engagement with the team during the meeting. Now what I think we miss when we fail to engage with someone directly is what they can add to the project in terms of value. Because I was not as vocal during the meetings, the executive assumed I wasn't knowledgeable about our business. He didn't see all of my contributions outside of the meeting, which in my estimation was where the real value was being developed.

When it came time to select who was going to support the oral presentation to the potential client, I was not included in the mix even though I had pretty much written the functional approach. Every presenter to the client was male; when we did internal reviews, the leadership team received some feedback stating we must have a more diverse team since the client leadership consisted of several females, including the main lead. Consequently, they asked me and another female who worked the proposal to participate, basically putting us in charge of the administrative items. I sat in the room and she worked the keyboard. While the team did well, it did not go without notice that its female members were relegated exclusively to an administrative role. Nevertheless, the client took it upon themselves to ask us questions, the answers to which we hit out of the park, much to the shock and delight of the lead executive. Afterward, the client stated that we were the ones who needed to make the presentation. Once we were back in the office debriefing, I also added my thoughts on our performance. The lead executive commented, "You really have a handle on this."

What I realized is that he made an assumption – whether based on conversations with his other cronies or his own perception – that I did not possess the knowledge to play a critical part in the oral presentation, nor did he make an effort to find out. It was also interesting to me that he was always comfortable going to those individuals with whom he had a working relationship but never seemed interested in extending that opportunity to others who could contribute just as well. So while there was a great deal left unsaid during this whole assignment, the entire experience taught me the necessity of making sure that others recognize the value of my contributions to the team.

True, the lead executive made an error by assuming a lack of knowledge on my part, but I neglected to go the extra distance in helping him realize that while others could talk a good game, they lacked substance, which impacted us during our oral presentation

– probably more than we even understood. Another emerging undercurrent was the fact that all of his cronies were guys; they ate lunch together, played golf together, and went to happy hour together. Whether he intended to or not, he sent a clear message to the women on the team. The good thing is that we did not win the work and the bad thing is that we did not win the work. There's an old adage that says, *know your audience*. In this case, the lead executive learned the importance of taking the time to know your client better. Had he assembled a more diverse team and employed the women in other roles besides administrative support, this story might have had a different ending. Whether the lead executive would have reached this conclusion on his own is not likely. For me, learning how to pay attention to the subtleties of these types of situations in the work environment is extremely important.

Difficult Conversations: The Art of Constructive Criticism

Over the course of my career, I have coached and mentored numerous people. What I have found is that I enjoy this aspect the most; I have also discovered that most people either don't know how to engage in a difficult conversation or avoid this kind of confrontation altogether out of fear. In my case, whenever executives in my company had to deliver a potentially upsetting message, they were clearly uncomfortable with initiating the conversation. To make the process flow more smoothly, I employed many tactics, like proactively starting off the conversation by mentioning the areas I knew could use improvement. When I removed the awkwardness, it became much easier to open up a productive dialogue. As a result, I made a conscious decision to ensure that I could participate in sensitive conversations with the individuals I counseled, coached, and mentored. Sometimes these sessions are extremely tough but I make an effort to put myself in their shoes. I'd always feel less valued when the conversation focused exclusively on the negative, or conversely, focused on nothing but the positive, leading me to believe everything was great when it was anything but that. So taking into consideration what I hated about such conversations, I developed my own strategy for delivering the right message.

As an executive in the consulting environment, one of your duties is being a career counselor. One year, I received a request to take on a new counselee that was in need of significant mentoring. Upon connecting with her, I tried to get an understanding as to the challenges she was facing. I had also done some research prior to our meeting in order to truly understand the situation and perception that surrounded her. I asked her to be as honest and open as she could to help me ensure we would focus on the right things. The conversation resulted in tears – not because I was harsh but because I listened and gave her direct feedback.

She basically stated she'd never engaged in such a direct, to-the-point dialogue. As a result of the first meeting, we established goals and objectives with regularly scheduled follow-ups to discuss the progress of her action plan. Many of the conversations required me to listen to the whole person and avoid jumping to conclusions or a solution without understanding the complete situation. In listening to her, I heard numerous things but most importantly, I realized she was facing similar challenges I had experienced over the years. I developed an immediate connection with her and knew I could help her move forward and find her own stride. What I also had to understand is that what may work for me may not work for her; whatever we did had to be tailored to her as a unique individual.

Another challenge we faced was assigning her to a new project that could give her somewhat of a fresh start. For this purpose, we continually worked together to move things forward, which involved talking about every one of her challenges but most importantly, helping her to develop different coping mechanisms she could employ when needed. I'm proud to say we managed to get her onto another project, where she followed her plan – the one we formulated together. Part of it entailed her discussing expectations and areas where she could add value with the project lead. We continued to work together on her strengths development plan. After closely collaborating for a year, the performance feedback she received was wonderful; she went from a low performer to a consistent performer. What was the main principle we worked on? You got it: communication. With my assistance, she learned how to set clear expectations on both sides and ensured that she understood how to manage through and up. Had I not cared enough to engage in a candid conversation with her, I'm not sure she would have remained with the organization. Since then, she has earned a promotion and continues to produce quality work.

Rumors Mills and False Expectations

Of the multiple aspects we may overlook with respect to communication, rumors top the list, mainly due to the negative effect they have on expectations. I've learned that if you do not push information out in a timely manner, most people will spend countless hours contemplating what they think is going to happen. When I first took over as the Assistant Adjutant General, many folks engaged in gossip – gossip about what I would do, what changes I would make, and how would I reconcile my new role with my civilian job. What bothered me the most is that individuals whom I'd known for years made assumptions regarding my decisions on personnel. If they'd taken the time to think about it, they would have remembered that I was never one who supported the status quo and would focus on organizational and process improvement. They never took into account the fact that I'd been assessing the team prior to taking over and identifying necessary changes. Still, I didn't make any announcements right away, preferring to deliberately understand my team's capabilities and strengths before taking action. During our first big leadership meeting, I clearly defined my vision, goals, and objectives with my key personnel in an effort to avoid any misunderstandings as to my expectations in terms of what to do and how to interact with me as their Commander.

During that first meeting, I gave them each a copy of the book, *Strengths Finder 2.0* and an assignment to send me their top five strengths – information I used as part of their assessment. Now up to this point, I felt I had been transparent on the direction in which I expected the team to move. I did not go into the assignment contemplating personnel changes but knew that could be a possibility, which was why I communicated to them my intention to analyze the key staff and determine whether or not their positions played to their strengths. When it came time for me to implement these personnel changes, some individuals expressed disappointment because they allowed their perception to drive their expectation, which was not aligned with what I'd communicated. I had never mentioned who would go where; therefore, none of them should have made assumptions.

These false expectations extended to the leaders on my team as well. Despite no indication from me, they felt absolutely certain I would move them into the specific positions they wanted, including the spot I was vacating. They even initiated conversations with staff pertaining to the changes they desired to make – before I had even left the seat! While I understand the urge to spread your wings and prepare for the next level, based on the way this was presented to me, these individuals were undoing actions I'd recently put into place. They were even having negative conversations about my decisions that in their minds, they needed to correct. Well last time I checked, these types of moves are not accomplished based on campaign promises. One thing I've learned over the years is that you may think that you can do better a job better than the individual in charge, but that attitude is not becoming of a leader or anyone else for that matter.

I say this as someone who has been guilty of the same behavior in the past: once upon a time, I used to think the same way but

I learned that while you may flourish in the job, even more than your predecessor, you are not justified in communicating your superiority in the role to others within the organization. Chances are, you might not have succeeded under the same circumstances. Even when you do get the opportunity to follow in someone's footsteps, it feels quite different from when you were on the outside looking in and making judgments about their competency. I have found that the job is invariably much more complicated than what I envisioned when someone else bore the full responsibility. Unless you are actually performing in a particular role, you cannot accurately anticipate the situations to which you will be exposed; therefore, do not count your chickens before they hatch. If you choose to do so, you may find yourself without a nest. When you do earn a promotion, it behooves you to express humility in declaring your intention to hopefully continue to move the organization forward. For my leader in question, I hope this was a teachable moment.

Communication at Its Finest

As I am sure you have experienced, we all have different ways of communicating; in some cases, it is passive at best. We typically bring unchecked emotion to the discussion, which puts us on the defensive or the fight-or-flight mode. We tend to get into standoff positions at opposite ends of the spectrum. Most of the time, we must figure out how to negotiate reasonable approaches to avoid saying what we think people want to hear and not what we really think. It is mind-boggling as to why we end up in such defensive positions but at the same time, it's puzzling that people feel they can say or do anything, regardless of how it impacts another human being. Sometimes we are so intent on getting our message across, we miss critical parts of the conversation. At the core of competent communication is the act of listening for the purpose of fully understanding before we render judgment. Case in point: it is not a hidden fact that Raj and I were raised to practice different religions. While others may view this as problematic, I would ask, *problematic for who?*

We completely understand our values and beliefs, and our faith in a Higher Power and each other is foundational to our relationship. We discussed our religious traditions early on and we both enjoy how we make it work. Now theoretically, this entire matter should have been settled just between the two of us, but it seems I had some family members who felt I no longer believed in God for whatever reason. I am not sure how they came to this conclusion but they made an assumption I had lost faith or lost my way. Regardless of how I tried to voice my point of view, they felt as if their position was correct.

In my mind, there are several things wrong with this scenario. First, they made an assumption based on some preconceived notion that I abandoned my faith. I am not sure where this misconception even came from. Secondly, I tried to share my perspective but it fell on deaf ears. Lastly, they felt as if their position or view was the only one. Here is what I would say to all of this: when we come into a conversation, we bring all kinds of biases with us – both knowingly and unknowingly. These biases prevent us from listening to and understanding one another, which are key components to good communication. In this mode, we are not fully engaged in the present moment. Instead of hearing the other person out, we're plotting our response.

In these discussions about religion, what I felt my family members were leaving unsaid was their belief that I was not going to reap the benefits of God because of my decision to marry a Hindu man. What totally fell short in this whole conversation was the conversation itself; in fact, there was *no* conversation, just a passage of judgment. I use this story to reiterate the critical component of listening in effective communication. The messages we send, whether verbal or nonverbal, will be perceived right, wrong, or indifferent. We must keep an open mind and remain nonjudgmental to the best of our ability when we communicate. Not doing so destroys our ability to have a constructive conversation and in fact, can harm our ability to build relationships, both personally and professionally. Enter conversations with the intent of being inquisitive about the other person, staying open to what they are saying and learning how to disagree or make a point without damaging the relationship. That does not mean you'll never experience times when tough, direct conversations must occur. The key point is to be mindful of another's position, avoid assumptions, ask questions, and always, always listen with the intention of being fully present.

CHAPTER 10

RESILIENT TO THE CORE – THE POWER OF FORGIVENESS

When I think back over my life, I'm amazed at how much progress I've made personally. At times, it's hard to believe that so much has happened to one person: me. I often look in the mirror, pinch myself, and think, *how long will this life that I now know is a blessing last?* You may be wondering how I managed to avoid feeling negatively toward those who have wronged me and how I made it this far without stopping. My answer? I was born with a wonderful ability to be resilient. While we can debate if resiliency is a gift bestowed upon a human at birth or a quality they must learn to develop over time, for me I don't see it any other way than as a natural part of my make-up. I did not have the breadth of experience in my teens to develop resiliency, so I have to believe that the characteristic is deeply embedded in my DNA.

Does It Ever Get Easier?

While it may seem (based on what I've shared) that things were always bad when I lived with my parents, that was not the case. For the most part, it was up and down. In those days, just like an addict, I had my good days and my not-so-good days. As a teen, it is hard to understand the challenges your parents may be facing or the experiences that have shaped them as people. Now with the wisdom of an adult, I often think about what was it like for my mother and father. Prior to moving in with them, I had only gotten a fleeting glimpse into their lives, which makes it difficult to envision their early years. It's a little easier with my dad; I can somewhat relate because I lived with his brothers and can't imagine that his experience in my grandparents' home deviated much from my own. While he did grow up in a slightly different period than the others, I'm fairly certain the environment remained the same.

As for my mother, I have absolutely no idea. I often think about whether her parents were loving and caring. *Were they distant with their affection? Was she afforded the opportunity to do the things she dreamed about doing?* I also wonder what it was like for her growing up as a beautiful young woman. From what she has told me, she never lacked for the attention of good-looking men, but I wonder about the things she has left unsaid, and whether they had an impact on the woman she became. I can't help questioning, *how did she meet my dad? What was it like to work in her field during a time in which race and gender were still significant issues?*

If I had the benefit of insight into these important aspects of her life, I know it would help me in my understanding of her as an individual. From the little bit she has shared, I realize that my mother has always been – and still is – as tough as nails. It seems she possessed an unbelievable ability to be resilient. As one of her three daughters, I know I would have benefitted from a discussion of this type of strength, if only my mother would have shared her life lessons with us. While you can watch what a person endures on a regular basis, it is not the same as listening to their stories of overcoming their own mistakes and challenges.

There were many strong women in my family who all played different roles in their households. Many of them worked outside of the home, at least, part-time. Since I grew up with this reality, it seemed normal; I never once questioned the need to work. I also knew that many of these women experienced hardships throughout their lives, but adding the responsibility for raising a family on top of that places each and everyone on a pedestal in my mind. My enormous respect for them extends to my mother. Mind you, none of this means I have no respect for the men in the family but it was expected that they would work to support their families: socially, this was their main function. In my family, it was the norm for everyone to play their part, which meant I sought to fulfill my responsibilities for my own reasons. In my estimation, this was the foundation for my strength. I learned early on that life was imperfect; you simply could not control the circumstances that would be thrown your way. As I watched my family overcome countless obstacles, I learned that when it was my time to deal with my own trials, I had to be strong in the face of adversity.

When I moved in with my parents, it never occurred to me that living with them would awaken a part of me I never knew existed. It was a new chapter in my life in which I had to learn how to begin to maneuver through tough times. This experience prepared me for the years to come, when my 'normal' life as a teenager would entail being on the street, not having a steady home, and drifting from place to place. As a result, I developed a remarkable ability to adapt to constantly changing circumstances. And although my decisions were not the best, at least, they were mine. I refused to dwell on the fact that I had to leave home, nor did I obsess about my looming early adult years, during which things would go from bad to worse. I just dealt with my problems as I confronted them. I learned to make multi-faceted plans so that if one thing didn't pan out, I had an alternative. It soon became second-nature to always think through every contingency based on the information available. In many cases, a lack of complete knowledge meant making less-than-optimal decisions. I can't say I didn't try to place blame where I felt justified; however, the desire to assign blame didn't necessarily plague my thinking day in and day out. I recognized that I was dealing with other underlying challenges.

The first started out with leaving home. Yes, the sexual assault crossed my mind occasionally but the bigger issue was leaving school; it was not yet apparent how the ramifications of the rape would manifest. When my uncle picked me up that evening, I think I stayed with him for a few nights until I made contact with my sister, Pam. It never occurred to me that I could live with him; I just wanted to be someplace where my parents couldn't find me. I didn't want to be forced to go back to the house and subject myself to more of the same. Therefore, the most pressing action I could take was to look ahead, not backward, and find another way to survive. It was a matter of choice.

The next decision I made months later was quitting school. I had dreams of going to college and had even looked at literature from several of the state universities. But I had no idea how I could afford it when I didn't know if I'd even be able to support myself financially through high school graduation, which was still a few years away. The reality of being homeless and barely making ends meet was much bigger than I ever imagined. *How had my family made things seem so easy?* How they'd made it to this point, I had no clue.

However, the one mantra my mother had driven into my head – the one I have never forgotten – was that education was critical. When I lived with her, she would make us read encyclopedias; little did I know this practice would stick with me well into my adult years. There was no doubt in my mind that education was important but I had no idea how I was going to rectify the situation until I went to Florida. I am not sure my parents ever knew I quit school. I couldn't tell you what they thought or where they believed I was living. *Did they care at that point? Did I even give a damn whether or not they were thinking about me?* I somehow got focused rather quickly on working to survive, which became a theme that would continue throughout my adult life. It's the reason why the opportunity to satisfy the need for education and work by joining the National Guard appealed to me.

When in the midst of these struggles and the ones I experienced as I got older, I never once believed they were insurmountable. I always believed I could overcome them, and that it was just a matter of time before the issue would go away, resolve itself, or inspire me to simply move on and leave it behind. I recognized I could do nothing to change my past circumstances, but I also knew I could look to a brighter day. Even while dealing with self-esteem issues, I continued to make progress and move forward. I never thought or expected it to be easy. When upsetting events took place, I'd roll up my sleeves and deal with them in the best way I knew how. A huge, sustaining factor in all of this was the presence of a support system in my life. Regardless of where I was or whatever was happening at any given moment, I gained strength from the support around me, whether it came from coaches, teachers, family members, friends, or acquaintances. At every stage of my life, I can assert this has been true. It should also be noted that I had an innate ability to consistently bounce back, learn from my failures, and simply move on. As I look back on my personal journey, the most challenging aspect was not overcoming adversity; it was cultivating my ability to forgive.

OMG Forgiveness, *Really?!*

I have no doubt many of you have experienced similar trials and tribulations at various points in your life. While the situation or circumstances may have been different, it's likely there are also plenty of similarities. Since I first began to share a snippet of my story with the public, I have been asked many questions, but the one theme that most frequently comes up focuses on forgetting and forgiving. I am not going to say I will ever forget my past and

I am not sure I even want to at this point. Whether good, bad, or just plain ugly, it's a part of me. For a while, some of the memories of the sexual abuse remained buried within. But as I've learned, traumatic experiences can bring them to the surface when you least expect it.

When I was first sexually molested, I did not recognize or even know what was actually happening. With young children, the reaction to such incidences can cause them to engage in unacceptable behavior that masks the underlying issue. Others may simply bury their feelings. For me, leaving my grandparents to move in with my parents was a traumatic event. It burned a mark into my soul that went deeper than even I understood. I developed all kinds of issues with self-esteem and confidence. It took several years for them to manifest into deep-seated problems I've spent most of my adult life confronting and counteracting. As a teenager, the situation that resulted in my father telling me to leave home shook me to my core. It threw me into an external battle with my parents and an internal battle with myself. It drove me to work hard to make my parents proud of me, even though it would not change the circumstances. I wanted to prove to them that I was better than they gave me credit for. I just wanted to make them and everyone else happy. Little did I know that this futile effort would only lead to making *me* unhappy in ways I couldn't comprehend. It meant that I was not living *for me* but out of a fear of disappointing others.

After I had finished my advanced individual training in Indiana, I was about four-and-a-half months pregnant and married. Mom and Dad allowed me to stay in their home for a few weeks until I could get a place in Frederick City closer to the hospital. My mother actually connected me with her cousin in Frederick, from whom I rented a room until I moved in with my sister Pam and her husband. They had a two-bedroom apartment, which afforded me more space. The point I am getting at here is that while my parents had thrown me out almost two years before, they seemed happy about the prospect of a forthcoming grandchild.

We did not talk about the incident that resulted in my leaving but I had also resolved I would never ever stay in that home again, *ever*, for fear of a reoccurrence. In the back of my mind, I never questioned my parents' intentions; I simply allowed them to be a part of my life again regardless of what had happened in the past. As the years have gone by, our relationship can best be described as a rollercoaster. Since allowing them back into my life, I have forgiven them time and time again. As crazy as it sounds, I have learned how to maintain a relationship with my parents, rather than divorcing them or shutting them out totally. No, it hasn't been easy, but I have realized there are many things for which I owe them my gratitude.

While I will never understand why they gave me to my grandparents, I can thank them for allowing me to receive the best when they could not give it to me, for whatever reason. There I had the privilege of being loved, learning essential values, and developing a genuine appreciation for a large family, something I would never trade for the world. I can thank them for trying to do the right thing by putting me into a home with running water and indoor plumbing. At the most basic level, I can truly thank them for bringing me into this world because without them, I would not be here at all. I may never get my questions answered and at this point, I am not sure it really matters. I can't deny that I love my parents even though I don't agree with the decisions they've made over the years. Still, they are a part of me and I can never erase that fact. Some way, somehow I have come to grips with the reality of who they are, but in the end, they are still my parents. If they need me or something else, I go to them without hesitation.

Being away from my family during my two deployments made me realize there are things that are much more important than holding onto anger, which only does you more harm than good. Constantly experiencing feelings of simmering resentment prevents you from moving on; it keeps you in victimhood mode and stops you from thinking positively about the future. During those deployments, I took the opportunity to work on the inner me and develop an inner peace. I took back control from that little monster that loves to make an appearance from time to time. My grandparents have both moved on from this world; I know they are in heaven watching over me and casting blessings my way. But my parents are still here, alive and well for me to continue to love them in a manner that works for me. Whenever they make the decision to jump back on that emotional roller-coaster, I let them do it, but I jump off. When their car comes to a complete stop, I am there to assist as they need. What I have come to realize is that I don't have to take that ride with them in order to love and, most of all, forgive them. Whether or not they love me unconditionally, I love them unconditionally and will continue to express my love for them for eternity.

You must be wondering about my brother. In the years following the sexual assault, I have not focused on what he did to me as you might understandably assume. Instead, I attempted to build a healthy brother-sister relationship with him. This too has also been an emotional rollercoaster. Remember when I briefly stayed with him after leaving my first husband, thinking things would somehow be different? Once I knew I'd been terribly mistaken, I jumped off the ride at the first possible moment. Over the years, he has visited my home on multiple occasions and although I was definitely guarded, I did not let that stop me from being a good host. My husband tells me I am too good-hearted, but I just remind him that he is my brother. I have forgiven him for all of his sins and just want him to find peace for himself. Clearly he has unresolved issues to reconcile, for which I am sorry. For way too long, I protected and harbored him from his crimes and now I realize I don't owe anyone anything; I don't have to protect those who have wronged me in ways that undermined my very existence. Long ago, I made a decision to keep my brother at arms' length, even though he'd call often and I would talk him. These conversations often elicited an uncomfortable feeling I just could not shake. Sometimes, they were borderline inappropriate, prompting me to make excuses as to why. Yet I also knew I couldn't continue to justify his behavior, actions, and intentions. He is who he is; I can't change that but I don't have to subject myself to his behavior either. Recently, he asked me if I was still mad at him. I assured him I'm not – I am just making a conscious decision to avoid interaction with people who want to make me feel inferior. I don't want to be with people, whether friends or family, who want to keep me on that emotional rollercoaster because they get off on the power it gives them. I told my brother I loved him, wished him the best, and hoped he has a truly blessed year.

I will continue to keep him at a distance and choose when and how we engage. Just because I have forgiven him does not mean I will ever give him the ability to exert any kind of control over me ever again. It does not mean that I have to be subjected to verbal assaults via text messaging or phone calls. It does not mean that I have to allow him to drag me through the mud because he doesn't understand why I talk about the rape instead of keeping it locked away in a closet. Finding the strength to discuss the events of that life-altering night has taught me valuable lessons. By sharing my story, I've learned that others have also found themselves in similar situations. I talk about trust, influence, control, powerlessness, and resiliency. But most of all, I talk about being a survivor and taking back control of my life by refusing to let someone else define me. You see, allowing myself to forgive him has freed me to move on with a healthy life. Despite the fact I had forgiven him decades ago, I had not summoned the courage to share my experience until 2012. You can't choose your family, but you can choose the what, how, and why you think of them the way you do. You can simply let it go and love them as they are.

For some, this may mean taking a similar approach as mine; for others, the best way of letting go and expressing unconditional love may involve cutting off contact altogether. Only you can decide the right path for you: the decision as to whether or not to physically keep people in your life who have hurt you, even after you've forgiven them, is unique to each individual. Either way, forgiveness does not translate into excusing the hurtful transgression. Rather, it's about releasing the pain you've been carrying around as a result of their actions so you can free yourself to live your life to the fullest.

Relentless 6

One of the most important life skills I've learned from my experience in the military is how to deal with adversity. When you wear the uniform and serve your country, you are constantly confronting challenging – and often life-threatening, situations. Therefore, you develop critical thinking skills out of necessity. I realized how well I'd absorbed these lessons when during my first deployment, I served as the division logistics chief for a team that was responsible for the movement, coordination, and all logistical functions for the deployment. This included personnel from 26 states. We trained up at the mobilization site, where we had to make tough decisions and work long hours. While there, we encountered several challenges which forced me to engage in helping my team.

As the senior ranking female, sometimes this assistance involved settling arguments among the female billets (a billet is a civilian's house or other nonmilitary facility where soldiers are lodged temporarily). Other times, it meant saying no to some crazy ideas that would have likely landed us in trouble. Regardless of the situation, I believe most would describe me as tough, reliable, willing to stand up to the team, and most of all, competent. A few of my counterparts from Massachusetts advised me I needed a call sign, but I was fairly certain that whatever they wanted to call me wasn't something I'd ever want to be repeated.

For whatever reason, I interacted the most with this particular team during the early part of the mobilization. One day, one of the guys bestowed me with the call sign, *Alpha Female*, which stuck with me for the duration of the deployment. To solidify the name, my deputy and a few others decided to present me with a hat that proudly displayed the words, *Alpha Female*. While I appreciated the gesture and the show of confidence, I wasn't crazy about the name. Still, I kept it until the end of the deployment.

When I became the Assistant Adjutant General, my Chief of Staff and I discussed the need for a call sign; I was adamant it would not be Alpha Female. So we spent a great deal of time brainstorming alternatives before we eventually came up with *Relentless 6* (the six stands for "commander"). I embraced the title wholeheartedly since my entire life theme centers around being relentless, the core foundation of resiliency. In order to build and develop resiliency, you must first exhibit relentlessness. My strong, unwavering belief in the necessity of being relentless compelled me to incorporate it into my leadership philosophy. Every individual and organization should strive relentlessly in their pursuit of excellence. To this day, I give out coins with the phrase *Relentless 6* engraved on them.

Put on Your Big Panties and Just Deal with It

It is important to realize we are in control of our own lives. We have the power to create our future. Once we acknowledge this truth, it is critical that we release emotions and experiences that weigh us down. At the same time, we must learn to express our feelings in a productive way that enables us to move on. For me, I revisit my past because it has shaped me into the woman I am today. It is part of me, but I now realize I was not defined by any particular situation or incident. Throughout my entire life, I've been blessed to have a support structure around me – whether my grandparents, my teachers in school, the West Frederick City families who welcomed me into their homes on those lonely nights, or the wonderful family that currently surrounds me.

My past ordeals have taught me innumerable lessons while empowering me to show the same kind of support to others. While I cannot change the situations and events that have transpired, I have overcome. I have moved on. As a well-adjusted adult, I can decide for myself my course of action when people try to drag me into their quagmires. True, I don't understand why some individuals engage in certain behaviors and I don't always agree with their actions, but I find forgiving them to be much easier than harboring bad feelings or continuing to beat myself up over what happened. Forgiveness is about getting unstuck and getting over it. Resilience is a critical part of the puzzle in that it gives us the strength to cope and deal with the challenges life throws at us. It gives us the power to choose to jump off or on the rollercoaster. It does not change what has happened but it can alter the way in which we perceive past and present events as well as ourselves. My life's experiences have taught me to be compassionate and to listen with intention. They have given me the ability to cultivate a keen sense of awareness with respect to decision-making skills that help me traverse any obstacle that lands in my path. They have permitted me to find a greater sense of purpose, one that is filled with peace and happiness. They have given me the power to be *Relentless to the Core.*

CHAPTER 11

FIRST IMPRESSIONS MAKE LASTING IMPRESSIONS

One evening when I was working in Afghanistan, one of the protocol liaisons approached my desk to ask if I would be willing to meet the first female Afghanistan General, Mohammadzai. They knew I was inspired by her story and accomplishments. She is a hero and role-model who consistently displays a level of courage others can only dream about.

When I met her, I could not help but smile from ear to ear. I couldn't contain my excitement since I'd never thought I'd ever have the opportunity to meet this extraordinary woman, who exuded confidence and charisma. Immediately, I felt welcomed by her. We chatted for a few minutes and took a photo together before she had to be escorted to her meeting with other senior leaders in the compound. I was a little taken aback when the translator relayed the message, "She would like to give you a hug," but I was surely not going to pass up the opportunity. When we embraced, I could truly feel the compassion. Then she stepped back to look at me and said something else which the translator repeated in English. It absolutely floored me when I heard his words, "She says you are genuine and pure at heart." At that point I was close to tears: *How is it that someone can look deeply into your soul and form an impression on which to base such a statement?* It was not the first time someone had made a similar remark about me while I was serving there.

In addition to my primary role, I also mentored an Afghan General from time to time. One day when I arrived at the Afghan National Army compound, he was finishing up a meeting when I walked into the room. He looked up and smiled at me as I smiled back. Dealing with him was a delight; I loved the fact that he did not seem to mind that I was a female and seemed genuinely interested in my opinion. He got up from his seat and introduced me to the others in the room while the translator gave me a full rundown of the conversation. As he made the introductions, he said: "This is my friend, and she is very genuine." Now keep in mind, while we talked about work and our families, having to communicate through a translator means you are essentially having a trilateral conversation. But again, it was an interesting thing to say, and it made me think about how your facial expressions, body language, and eye contact have a remarkable effect on how others see you. While I have always known this to be the case, these comments caused me to reexamine my actions to ensure that I extend the same level of comfort to everyone I meet. It also revealed that my smile was definitely contagious. With this knowledge, I took pride in greeting everyone with a sincere smile. This was a lesson I had difficulty learning in my early adult years when I believed it was better to keep a straight face in order to be taken seriously. Back then, I found it was easier to hide behind that image regardless of what was going on in my life.

Here's another view about the impression you make on people when you first meet them, or even when you see them in passing. Working in the joint operations center in Kabul was a job that could weigh you down if you let it. You'd be mostly indoors all day in a large room with hundreds of people working on their computers – individuals from many countries who were focused on the day's activities. Since there were no windows, we were deprived of natural light, which the not-so-great indoor lighting could not compensate for. We were always serious about our work, which is a good thing, but sometimes you just have to elevate the mood. On a regular basis, I'd receive tons of care packages from my civilian employer as well as friends and family. My civilian employer sent shipments almost every month – and I'm not talking one small box. On average, they'd ship about 10 boxes filled with a wide variety of goodies. I would share the contents with everyone on my team and those who were in the joint operations center because it was the least I could do. We had several Afghans working there, and I would put aside baby wipes and chocolate for them. As a result of this simple gesture of kindness, one day they brought me a cup of chai tea, knowing it was my favorite. Another time, I encountered two soldiers from Greece walking toward me, so I smiled and rendered the greeting of the day. I extended this courtesy to everyone because wearing a smile on my face as much as possible made my day brighter. I remember the day the Greek soldiers stopped to tell me they just wanted me to know that when I say hello and render the greeting of the day to them, they like that I am always smiling. They said, "I hope you don't mind us saying this, but you light up this place with your smile, and it makes us also want to smile. It is contagious, so please keep it up." I thanked them and promised I would do my best to remember, regardless of the kind of day I am having. You never know how your words and actions affect other people, but you should always keep in mind that a smile, just like a picture, is worth a thousand words in many cultures.

A Matter of Survival

When I first joined the military, I was in need of something to guide, shape, and mold me. I did not know whether or not it would work for me, but making the choice to join was purely based on the need to survive. Therefore, when the opportunity presented itself, I did not give it a second thought. I learned that when you take advantage of the opportunities that come your way, many more choices appear. Often, we are so caught up in our troubles and woes that we don't possess the right level of self-awareness. We then can miss the best things in life that may have been right there in front of us. I'm not suggesting that every opportunity is perfect, but if you don't first recognize it and then harvest the benefits that are usually just below the surface, you have wasted the chance. I also learned that letting others dictate my choices usually resulted in a worse position or, at the very least, have to do something or be someplace I absolutely hated. After leaving my ex-husband and coming off of an inactive military period into the Army Reserves, I continued to serve out my enlistment contract. I found that after being inactive, I truly missed the military; the only reason I'd left was to be with my husband. Coming back after that break was tough. As I previously highlighted, I had trouble making my drills for several years, but when I was at drill, I worked. Yes, I did it because I liked it but also because I desperately needed the money. It was a necessity for me to get a drill check, which made the difference between having to choose among putting food on the table, paying the rent, or buying needed amenities.

Somewhere along the path, it transformed from being a method of survival to being a portal to limitless opportunities. It was clear that I was willing to do anything I could to make things better for my family and advance to a much better position. Through this process, I found that reinvention referred to more than just the work I was doing. It was through this process that I made the choice to go back to traditional school and officer candidate school, both of which focused on education and learning. Within a very short period, I found that things were coming full circle. I had no idea how I was going to get my education and – poof! – the opportunity appeared. It was at a time in which I could barely make ends meet, but somehow it became a reality, even though I remember thinking there was no way I could afford to go to school. It is now clear that one of my traits is the ability to take action: I have never been afraid to take a chance even when the odds were against me. In the corporate world, this is known as "rebranding" or defining your brand to create your future. But at the time, that concept was not apparent to me. I simply considered it to be a matter of survival.

Going through officer candidate school with the Maryland National Guard, the leader in me truly started to emerge. There again, things came full circle because the Maryland Guard is where I started about ten years before. Once I became an officer, my thinking about the military significantly changed. It shifted from being a necessity to being something I thoroughly enjoyed. Since then, I don't think I have ever missed a drill without having a plan in place to make it up. It has become part of me, although I wonder if it had *always* been a part of me. Maybe I'd never acknowledged that my passion for the military had been running through my veins, just as surely as my blood. Consequently, when called upon to serve my country abroad, I took the leap of faith and put all else in God's hands. To tell you the truth, I had taken a leap of faith many times before, and God had guided me through.

Finding Your Passion

Multiple opportunities came my way in 2013. While I had to make some tough decisions, it was really about discovering where they would take me. The journey never seems to be dull, and one of the lessons I've learned is that you must be prepared for anything to happen. I had taken over as the Director of the Joint Staff for the Maryland National Guard around the fourth day of Hurricane Sandy, which allowed me to right-seat left-seat ride with the existing director. After having been in the role for five months, I was promoted to Brigadier General. In the summer, I was asked to consider becoming the Assistant Adjutant General running the Army side of the Maryland Guard – a discussion I was not expecting, especially since I was working full-time. I was taking on the role someone else had filled full-time, but I needed to figure out how to fulfill the same responsibilities while working part-time. While it was definitely a challenge, I rose to the occasion.

In fact, we established a battle rhythm that actually worked well. In spite of my not being there full-time, we accomplished much. It was critical that my schedule was well coordinated and that I set a vision with strategic direction. I had to balance between many activities I enjoyed. I spent most weekends doing unit visits, observing training, and meeting with the leaders in the field while continuing to set the direction for my team. Even though this is a higher level command position, spending time with the troops helps to keep me grounded – maybe because I was enlisted for a period of time. After spending time with them, it was not hard to remember why I do it. I felt as if I was in heaven. I had found my stride again in my civilian job and was reveling in the role of being a commercial director, focused on operations within one of our portfolios. This was the key position I assumed right after returning from deployment.

At first, I wasn't thrilled about it but what I think truly changed my outlook was the fact that I felt was I was making an impact – something highly important to me regardless of my role. The other thing that made a difference? I had started coaching and mentoring again in my civilian role, which closely mirrored my interactions with the troops. Coaching others also gave me a feeling of being grounded and balanced. At no time did I ever feel overwhelmed; on the contrary, I seemed to thrive in both worlds. I believe this marked the beginning of something wonderful. Not that I am indicating that my prior life was less than stellar, just that this experience was a catalyst for something different. One of my coworkers, who was the diversity lead for our organization, told me that my purpose for being on this earth was something greater than anything that has happened to me thus far and that the greatest part was yet to come.

To this day, I have reflected on that comment over and over, using it to help me define what I am truly passionate about. Taking the role as Assistant Adjutant General came with many nuisances I had not considered. I did not realize it would garner so much attention. My friends, family, soldiers, airmen, and the community celebrated this achievement for months on end. As one of my friends, who is also a general officer, complimented, "You are one of one, you are our star." I had no clue what he was referring to and had to ask for clarification. He pointed out that in the Army Guard, I was the only African-American female general officer. As I read his email reply, it hit me: *this was no longer about me.* Nothing that I would or could do from here on out is about me; it is bigger, *much* bigger. The concept was overwhelming. At that point, I had no idea what it would really mean. I knew that everything I did from here on out had to take into consideration what being selected for this role would mean to others. It also meant that my life had purpose beyond anything I could have ever imagined.

As I continued to enjoy being the Assistant Adjutant General, another twist came my way with my civilian employer. I received a call asking if I was interested in being considered for the Director of Operations for the North America Health and Public Service operating unit, with estimated revenues of $3 billion. After working solely in an operations role for the portfolio, it was a natural next step. Obviously, I replied, "Yes, I would like to be considered." After I had hung up the phone, I informed my husband I had no idea what I'd just gotten myself into, but to be prepared for another major change.

When I was selected for the role after a thorough interview, I knew it was a position that would afford me a chance to step out of my comfort zone as I grew into it. It was most definitely a stretch. However, I thought about the individuals I mentored to take on challenges and break out of *their* comfort zones and realized it was time for me to take my own advice. My new role required me to move from our federal group to the commercial side of our organization – the functional areas of our business I had not been focused on. While federal was still part of the overall group, the health and state/local business units required me to come up to speed in order to understand our business in these areas. I put on my learning cap and just went for it. Going in, I focused on the tasks I naturally did well and began to establish those areas. This approach allowed me to then focus on the areas in which I had to develop a deeper business understanding. On top of this, I also worked with our leadership team on the rollout of a new operating strategy, business systems, and processes, which was an ongoing project for the next year. Taking on this additional responsibility meant I was working hard to be successful in two different career paths in two major organizations. I did not relinquish my executive sponsorship roles with organizations that focused on veterans' initiatives because they were much too important to me. I also remained fully engaged in our diversity initiatives. Clearly, I was living the dream – one that I never envisioned. Still, the events of the next year would prove I had absolutely no idea as to what was to come.

In August of 2014, the Adjutant General for Maryland announced he was planning on retiring at the start of the new administration. He explained the process they would employ to provide useful information to the new administration in determining his replacement, and encouraged the qualified officers to throw their names in the hat when the time was right. I debated for months as to what I was going to do and included my husband and daughters in the decision process. Achieving this next milestone meant that for the first time ever, I would be in uniform full-time. It was a significant shift in focus, but one that deep down, I knew I needed to make if given the opportunity. I was aware that there were many talented individuals who would also be considered, but I also knew much depended upon what that the administration was seeking. I was not politically connected to any of the candidates for Governor, which could be viewed as good or bad. I had a strong resume that reflected a diverse background, and my organization had strong performance results tied to the strategy, goals, and objectives I'd established. In other words, I had a proven track record: I had to believe it was enough to at least get them to consider me.

Shortly after the Maryland elections, I had the chance to make an important presentation to the transition team. Knowing how much was riding on it, I ensured that I made the best impression possible. When I got the call for the interview, it was clear to me that things were about to get real: I was going to meet with the newly elected Governor Larry Hogan and his Chief of Staff, Dr. Craig Williams. After the interview, I called my husband and announced, "I really like this guy, and if I am asked to take this role, I would have a hard time saying no."

On December 22, 2014, the Governor called to offer me the job as Adjutant General. I remember exactly how I felt. I had just left the office that was reviewing my security background and reached my car, filled with nervous energy as I wondered if they'd select me. But when I got the call, I already knew the answer. It was my destiny, my chance to impact an organization that had done so much for me – one I could not and did not want to ignore. I'd been given the opportunity to lead the organization that had taken me off the streets as a scared teenager over 34 years prior; it was time for me to repay the debt. As far as I was concerned, nothing less than the ultimate sacrifice of leaving my consulting career behind to serve a higher order would do.

The 91st Day

Little did I know, the first 90 days would be absolutely crucial. As I was standing at the entryway to the Governor's mansion on the 21st of January 2015, it felt a little surreal. I was prepared to escort the newly elected Governor and the First Lady of the State of Maryland, Ms. Hogan, into the State House for the swearing-in. We were getting ready to make the final walk, which had profound meaning for me because it was also my first official day as the Adjutant General of Maryland. Even though I knew I earned the distinction through my own on accomplishments and competence, it was a significant milestone for more than just me. I was the first African-American *and* the first female Adjutant General for the state. In fact, nationwide at this point in time, there had only been two females prior to me. What stood out to me was that I was actually creating history. *Who would have ever thought that after coming from such a challenging life, a reward such as this would be waiting?*

I never imagined in a thousand years I would end up in this position. That day, I recall waiting and preparing to move; I felt nervous but tried my best not to let it show. Although this was not my first inauguration, it was the first in this capacity. *What if I tripped or did something stupid that would end up on camera for that day?* I tried to give the Governor and Ms. Hogan the most reassuring smile I could muster. When we started the walk, I tried to remember the lessons I'd learned from all of my training up to this magnificent point in time. I knew how to do this. I knew how to keep things moving in the right direction. My focus remained on the overall goal as I tried to ensure that I did all of the right things.

Once we got into the reception area, I could relax for a short time before I had to perform my function of knocking on the chamber doors to announce the Governor and the Maryland First Lady. I'm pretty sure I knocked too hard because they clearly heard it, then I announced their entry in a loud command voice – all the while thinking to myself, *please don't forget what you are supposed to say.* It was less than fifteen words, but it might as well have been an encyclopedia entry. After getting through it, I could then only watch the swearing-in on the screen. While I was watching, I realized that one of my folks, who'd been chartered with the care of the Bible for the ceremony, was still on the platform during the swearing-in and signing. Protocol dictated that they step away out of range of the cameras. However, the concept of being *present but invisible* had obviously not resonated with this officer. Ugh! I just knew that this incident would come up at a later point, and the only thing I could think about was how much I wanted to crawl under a table and die. This was not supposed to happen.

As much as we would like to think otherwise, we cannot always control the actions or reactions of others. I had to simply let it go for the moment and stay focused on the task at hand. I had to be present and in the moment. And I wanted to *enjoy* the moment. Once the ceremony was completed inside, I escorted them outside for the address speech. As I showed them to their places, I was amazed at all of the people in attendance, including my entire team, which was there to provide logistical support including security, traffic control, and escorts. Everything seemed to be perfectly in place. Watching this unfold was an amazing, picturesque moment. As the Governor started his speech, the snow began to fall. To top it off, the day finished with the inauguration ball, which my husband and I both attended. It was the perfect ending to one of the most beautiful and memorable days in my entire life to date.

In the days that followed, I had to shift my focus to the organization and think about what I needed to put into place. Thankfully, my predecessor and I had a chance to discuss the transition in detail, and he allowed me to begin stepping into the role early in January. I had already made some assessments in the months prior and was able to confirm my thoughts and perceptions while talking over the immediate challenges I would need to handle right out of the gate. The first order of business was ensuring we had an up-to-date strategic plan that was nested from the highest level down to the lowest. The key in providing effective guidance to the team was making it a living plan, no more than twenty pages. I wanted the information to be clear but realistic so that anyone could understand the vision and direction for the organization based my directives. I worked with my team to define what I wanted to have in place at the end of the ninety days, which I considered to be my transition period. Throughout the process, it became evident that my business skills were absolutely applicable to everything I was preparing to do. Furthermore, my consulting skills had also prepared me well for building the necessary schedule of activities during the ninety days. While I focused on the current organization, I also determined if I needed to make leadership changes. If so, I wanted to do that extremely early in the cycle, for numerous reasons.

The good thing was that I was not new to the organization. I had been observing processes and activities for almost eighteen months as the Assistant to the Adjutant General (ATAG). I knew the leaders and their strengths, personalities and past performance. This knowledge provided me with great insight to the leadership moves I needed to consider. Instead of making hasty decisions, I decided to conduct interviews to fill my replacement as well as the new ATAG Air. This meant the two top key positions below me would need to switch out. At first, the thought of it made me somewhat nervous, but the more I deliberated about it, the more I realized it was the perfect time to make changes while simultaneously setting a different leadership tone reflective of the direction in which I wanted to take the organization. This was the one action all of my predecessors had suggested I take.

Although I had originally planned on taking it slowly, it became apparent that it was best to make the shifts with every key position. I contacted several general officers from outside of the state to ask them to help me pick my new leadership team. I opened up the advertisement for both positions nationwide. Every action I took was done for the purpose of finding the best possible officers. I firmly believe in the old adage, "Cream rises to the top," yet I knew that many believed my approach was a slap in the face to my current general officers. However, that was never my intention. I truly wanted to guarantee to the best of my ability that I made the best selection for the organization.

The board I pulled together was comprised of four general officers with diverse backgrounds from different organizations: The Commander of the District of Columbia National Guard; the National Guard Bureau Special Assistant; the Deputy Commander of 1st Army; the State Director of Homeland Security; and my Chief of Staff as the recorder. I felt this was a very experienced group for which I would receive the best recommendation possible. Once we had the list, I had to make a decision on the leadership moves we'd have to make. It was clear that doing so would cause a ripple effect because any change to the current staff would result in a secondary move. That's why I contemplated the reorganization carefully, taking into consideration each individual's personality as well as their capabilities. While I understood that the new assignments would not necessarily satisfy everyone, it was not a factor in my decision-making. By the time I made my choices and sent out the notifications, I was almost ninety days into my term. With the leadership team in place and a vision beginning to take shape, we were already on a good glide slope. However, just when things seemed to be going well, the civil unrest in Baltimore kicked off. Well...so much for a smooth transition. I love the book, *The First 90 Days* and have used it for role transitions; now was I was using it for a job transition. What's good about it? The book is a simple and realistic guide to developing a plan for your first 90 days. What was the downside? The civil unrest in Baltimore happened on the 91st day.

Civil Unrest

In April of 2015, I was in Boston attending a senior executive level course on Homeland Security with many other general officers and local government officials. The curriculum focused on case studies and discussions about crisis-planning in situations that always begin locally before escalating. Our session centered around responses to events like 9/11, Katrina, and even Ferguson, which were used as the backdrop to strategize about our responses to similar crises. Attending the course sparked a multitude of thoughts about riot-control planning in Maryland. We had just completed our exercise for this response plan in the fall of 2014, but for some reason, my intuition was alerting me to pay close attention to the lessons. I asked my team to review in detail the Ferguson scenario, along with any takeaways from the riots of 1968. While I trusted and acted upon my inner wisdom, I didn't as yet understand why these preparations were necessary to undertake at that moment. Perhaps not so coincidentally, this course took place almost two weeks before the Baltimore incident was even a glimpse in our minds. I kept sending emails to my team, and I am certain they were scratching their heads thinking, *what is she worried about? Why is she asking so many questions? Why is she so focused on riots?*

I was sitting in my office in Baltimore the Friday before the funeral for Freddie Gray, watching the news periodically to monitor the situation. I'd already instructed my team to renew things and get in touch with their counterparts to ensure we'd be ready if we saw anything that gave us cause for concern. This included looking at our logistical situation for equipment and troop staging. When the Emergency Manager and Superintendent of the State Police asked if they could stop by to see me, I knew my intuition had been spot-on. Our discussion focused on what we'd need to do if events turned ugly. By the time they left my office, I was in full action mode and on the phone with my Director of Joint Staff. I asked them to lean as far forward as possible while remaining just short of a National Guard call-up. I determined that we needed to be ahead of the curve because civil disturbances can escalate more quickly than we can respond. I asked them to begin unit alerts to posture us for the most rapid response we could muster. I also requested that they tap into our relationships at the local level for the purpose of ensuring we were as connected as we could possibly be.

We continued to monitor the situation all through the weekend but still did not lower our posture because I felt that we needed to get past the funeral before we could be sure that things would not intensify. I continued to communicate back and forth with the Director of Homeland Security for our state. We remained in close contact throughout the weekend and especially on the Monday of the following week. In the aftermath, many folks have repeatedly asked if I would change anything or do anything differently while others have inquired about my ability to remain calm and focused. Well...when I think about how the situation unfolded for our activation, it was clear I had to rely on all of my previous training and experiences. While responding to civil unrest was not an experience in my toolkit, I have worked in many joint operations centers and planning cells, and I can state with confidence that my leadership skills are among my core strengths. When dealing with these types of situations, you have to quickly sift through the catalog of experiences in your brain to access the right tools to be used. As I began to gain situational awareness, I recognized the importance of specific relationships with respect to the unfolding events. I understood how crucial it was that my message conveyed the right advice when speaking with the Governor or local leaders; that the direction I gave my team was clear; and that I fully understood who I needed and where I needed them.

A multitude of thoughts reverberated through my mind on that Monday, and I just went into action. At no time did I second-guess myself; I relied on and trusted that I'd put all of the right tools in place in order to deal with the event as a leader. After all, the Governor had hired me to lead and advise in every type of situation. I was trained for it and the community needed me to stand strong in the face of a different kind of adversity. *Essentially, hadn't my life prepared me for this all along?* I knew how to be compassionate and how to connect with our citizens. I have been in their place, where you feel wronged by a system that is not supporting you. I knew that sense of loss and tension, based on the struggles I'd confronted throughout various portions of my own life. If there's one thing that helped me the most during this challenging time, that was it. Because I had a critical job to perform, I understood there was no place for my opinion; I had to deal exclusively with the facts. I also knew I needed to demonstrate a level of compassion and understanding until everything was resolved.

When events began to spiral out of control that Monday, I knew it was a matter of time before I was heading into the operations center to meet with my boss and the team. I was ready. More importantly, my team was ready to execute and make history again. We were activated for civil unrest, which had not happened in Maryland since the 1968 riots. In preparing for the very first press conference, I realized whatever I said would be repeated by media; therefore, words mattered. I had to set the tone for the Guard response for the sake of our citizens and my troops. This was not some faraway place in another country; this was our community in which we lived and worked. These people were our families, friends, coworkers, associates, and our children. In many cases, they were us.

My messages to my team were crystal-clear in this aspect: we must and will treat everyone with a level of respect, but we will ensure that we protect people and property to the best of our ability. We were there to support the local authorities and as such, we were not to forget our place and our role. As events unfolded that evening, I thought for sure I would be fired as tensions rose and we had not gotten our folks on the street. Many circumstances were problematic, but timing of our response was critical. Looking back, I surmise that many that had not seen me get into full Generalship mode, directing the order of events that needed to occur because initial coordination between agencies can be difficult. I will not say I completely lost it, but I will say that my patience meter was fully pegged by 2100 hours that evening. I had to do everything I could to take a step back and not allow what we were seeing on TV to drive my decisions. It was my job to guarantee that communications between my team and the local law enforcement team were fully integrated. Once our HUMVEES carrying our initial response force rolled down North Avenue, you would think I would have been relieved, but for me, it was an excruciatingly tense point in time. I had been watching the response and feared that if this effort to support the local authorities failed to calm to the madness, it would get real ugly pretty quickly. I closed my eyes and began to say a silent prayer asking for assistance, for calm, and to get people to go home. My prayers, as I am sure many others, were answered. Things quieted down significantly that evening. We could in no way rest easy, but tomorrow would be a new day with fresh challenges we'd deal with as they came.

Synergy – All Things Come Full Circle

As that week progressed, we mobilized over 3,000 troops between the Army and Air National Guard. The days were long, and I am truly not sure how much sleep I got throughout the entire ordeal. My role required me to bounce between the state and local levels for coordination in order to continue to move things forward. Relationships with all parties were an essential element; I would even say that one of my most important tasks to date continues to involve fostering cooperative relationships with our state and local authorities. Bouncing between the different levels and dealing with my team on some days was grueling. Whenever I reached a level in which I needed to get away to refocus, I would go out to do circulation where I could interface with my soldiers, airmen, and police officers.

However, I never made these rounds without talking with the officers out there on the street – an activity I deemed critical in the overall scheme of things. One day during that week I went out to visit my airmen down at the Inner Harbor. Since the weather was beautiful, I decided that a walk from our base to that location would do me good. My security team, Command Sergeant Major, and Public Affairs Officer accompanied me on this visit. It was important to me to personally thank as many of our folks as I possibly could. Additionally, I wanted to remain visible, which I believed was vital. Unexpected events transpired during these visits – events that reinforced the fact that we were making a difference. As we were coming back, a boat cruise was unloading at the Inner Harbor. I turned to look at my team and instructed them, "Let's just walk to the outside and get past the folks unloading."

What I never anticipated was for one of the ladies to recognize me and announce in a loud voice, "It's her, it is Major General Singh." I wasn't sure what was going to happen next, but I greeted her with a smile, which prompted approximately 60 women to surround me. I thought my security team was going to have a cow as these women hugged me, said little prayers, asked to take selfies with me and thanked me for everything our troops were doing to help their community. I stayed with them for about 20 minutes, and it was well worth the time. Somehow, I felt refreshed by the interaction, lighter even, if you can believe it. Peace washed over me and calmed me; it carried me through to the end of the civil disturbance. As I continue to reflect back on that event, I have never once questioned my commitment or loyalty to our nation or our citizens. When you are passionate about what you do, it shines through all else. When you enjoy selfless service, good will prevail. Starting a career with the Maryland National Guard in 1981 as a homeless high school dropout, to commanding the organization that essentially saved me from a life on the streets to helping local authorities, to saving one of our communities, is where everything came full circle for me. There is no possible way to know what life has in store for you, but one thing is guaranteed: there is a plan.

CHAPTER 12

LIFE'S PLAN – STUFF HAPPENS

I have been asked many times: *How did you do it? Did you have a plan? How did you know what decision to make?* Thinking back to when I was a homeless 16-year-old who'd just quit school, I'd have to say I didn't have a plan. I'd had no intention of leaving home, nor could I have ever anticipated the circumstances that led to my father telling me to go. As a consequence, I simply drifted from day to day, too stunned by what had occurred to worry about what was going to happen beyond the next 24 hours. In fact, the only thing I *could* think about back then was my present situation.

However, I also knew that my dire circumstance would not be permanent. Precisely how I knew it, I'm not sure, but I had to believe that my life could and would change. I also realized if I wanted a favorable outcome, I had to do something different. Later, upon returning from advanced individual training with a baby, I understood the necessity of formulating a plan. I envisioned myself in a specific profession, which was not where I ended up. Lacking a solid foundation, it was up to me to determine how I was truly going to make it from here on out. And yet, even at that point, I still had no clue. The reality is that life has so much more in store for us than we can ever imagine; the key lies in accepting the opportunities that come your way. From there, use the ones that serve you best to build your foundation.

Think of a tree that begins to grow from a small seedling. Once it begins to sprout and the roots start to grow, the foundation is still fragile. As the tree continues to mature, its foundation expands, and its branches begin to grow in all directions. This is not only representative of my life but yours as well. During those first five or so years on my own, my foundation was extremely fragile until I started to gain more and more experience; I would take one path only to discover a perceived dead-end. Once I learned to plan well, I realized that while one particular branch might lead to nowhere, I could usually jump to another one. This new branch represented a fresh opportunity to move forward. For me, thinking in terms of a tree as a symbol for my life makes sense.

When I was a young girl, I always wanted to climb trees to see just how high I could get. No matter how many times I climbed the same tree, I would experiment with different paths to discover which one would lead me to the highest heights. Once I discovered the best paths, I eventually made it to the top. In fact, the only tree I left unconquered in our yard was the big walnut tree because I didn't have the necessary skills or tools for success. What I love most about this tree metaphor is that it highlights the many paths any one person can take. One note of caution: it is important to realize that every individual embarks on their own unique journey and holds their own views and opinions. We, in turn, should respect and value those differences – even if they are vastly different than our own.

Roots and Foundation - Where Are You?

Upon discovering the National Guard, I realized I had options I never knew existed. This was promising. At that point in time, I did not know anything about food stamps or welfare (which I did find out about years later). I've never signed up for these services even though at times I truly needed them. Okay, I am sure you are thinking, *Linda how did you not know about such things?*

Welfare was never discussed in my family. And since my grandparents and parents never used it, it was not familiar to me. What *was* familiar was to work hard for whatever you wanted. Working seemed natural. The day I enlisted in the National Guard, I developed hope. My prospects started to look up. While I still didn't have a place of my own, many friends were there to support me. In fact, I landed a job about three months before I left for basic training because of one of my friends who worked at Airpax told me they needed help. She felt confident that I could get on the evening shift in one of the departments. This was a huge development because I needed the money. However, taking the job meant leaving the pretzel shop. Together, my friend and I worked on my thin resume, and she gave me an excellent reference. I highlighted the skills I'd gained from the electricity and electronics classes in high school since the plant focused on various electrical parts. With her support, I landed the job.

The only problem?

Since I was scheduled to ship to basic training, I had no choice but to leave a few months later. In reflecting back on the experience, I'd say that while it was not a well thought out plan, it was a plan nevertheless, and a choice I could live with. Let's face it: taking this job enabled me to meet one of my basic necessities – money to survive. It provided an excellent transition into the military component, which went above and beyond in that it met several of my needs including money, career, fitness, health and service. In considering the process of building a foundation and satisfying vital necessities, in my estimation, the military was the better choice. While I'm positive that undergoing this mental exercise was completely unintentional (I had no clue that I was actually engaging in a planning exercise), I did it. Regardless of whether or not it was done haphazardly, I accomplished my goal.

Returning from basic and advanced individual training and moving to Florida, on the other hand, were intentional choices. Once in Florida, I truly started thinking about purposefully planning my actions and building upon my foundation. I not only gained more experience, but I also had a family unit around me that helped open my eyes to many other possibilities. Extended family has always been important, but this move helped me understand just how significant a family's role is when things get tough. My then mother-in-law and her sister played an incredible role in my growth during this period, assisting me in reconnecting with my spiritual life and focusing on self-development. My mother-in-law honed in on a key aspect: earning my high school diploma. Together, we worked toward that goal.

Once my husband returned from overseas, our plan was to live and raise our daughter in Florida. When circumstances took a turn for the worse, I made another plan to leave him. However, as a result of failing to think it all the way through, I had to deal with unanticipated second-and-third-order impacts. It was harder to reestablish myself for numerous reasons, but mainly what I learned from the experience is that every step in a plan is essential. For example, I neglected to prepare myself by establishing a good credit history. The only credit I had was with my ex, which was not very much. Therefore, it was almost impossible to buy a crucial, big-ticket necessity like a car. This was a significant lesson because it took me years to establish my credit, something I didn't fully appreciate until I needed it.

Returning back to Maryland and working in the metropolitan area was the most significant move I could have made in my early twenties. My growth at this time was slow and challenging, but I continued to focus on all of the areas I thought were most important. As I gained new experiences, built new relationships, and accessed more knowledge, my desire to do these things grew exponentially. When not engaged in these personal and professional growth efforts, I found that I was not happy because the result was a stagnant life. Once you realize you are both mentally and physically taxed, you then need to consider the necessary steps to reinvigorate yourself.

At this point, I had developed enough knowledge and had a good enough support system around me to understand at least some of what it would take to make effective decisions. This does not mean everything fell right into place, but my life did seem to progress. I established credit and landed a job that helped me develop my skills – skills that served as the fibers that allowed me to widen my base. My main focus was on developing myself spiritually, physically, and mentally. This is an ongoing, never-ending process; something I continue to focus on to this day. No matter how much you accomplish, you should never get too comfortable but rather, constantly strive to be the best you that you can possibly be. When you are analyzing your foundation and determining where to place your focus, you should consider all aspects of your life. Think broadly in order to have a full view of the whole you, which encompasses family, spirituality, self-reflection, self-development, health, fitness, career, and finances. Keep in mind that where you are today can be temporary if you want it to be. But before you can begin to look at the options, you absolutely must come to terms with the here and now. This is the first step toward gaining awareness into you.

Branches and Sequels - Identifying What Is Important to You

As you can imagine, my life was not straightforward. There was no clear path I could take in order to get out of any one situation. Even when I was working back in the DC area, I felt as if I was constantly falling from one branch to a lower branch, or sometimes two branches lower. Disappointments occurred due to poor decision-making while others may have also been inevitable. What I learned at this point in my life is that if I wanted different outcomes, then I had to take different actions. In order to do that, I had to figure out what mattered most to me: Was it men, drinking, and hanging out? Working? Taking care of my daughter? Going to school? Or going back to the streets?

I had to get real with myself and come to the realization that the life that I was leading was not going to lead me to the place I envisioned. After that, finding a decent job became a priority, and I seemed to be fortunate in my ability to maintain steady employment. Securing work that would go beyond taking care of the necessities and provide a financial cushion was of the utmost importance. What you may not realize is that it took me 14 *years* to get to that point. That encompassed 14 years of frequent challenges, long nights, homeless nights, lonely nights, and uncertainty. In 1988, I focused on my priorities with laser precision; what I found was that in the beginning, they would change often. Some were short-term, i.e. enrolling Shaniece in a good school, while others were long-term, i.e. finishing my bachelor's degree.

These 14 years of hard knocks taught me much about prioritizing what is truly most important. During the earlier years, work, childcare, money, food, and a solid roof over our heads were the most pressing priorities. While they remained important, once I developed an unshakeable foundation, my focus then turned toward education for both my child and me. I knew that without somehow obtaining my degree, I would have to work two, three, and maybe even four jobs until she graduated from high school. Some days, I would work all day, pick her up from the childcare provider, fix dinner, feed and bathe her, and take her back to spend the night. I would then either go to class or my evening job, which meant I would not see her until the next evening because I also had to work the next day. I was working myself into a frenzy and could not see beyond the next tree coming my way. While it may be admirable to take on all of these goals, it created a poor quality of life. At that point, I started getting focused and serious about my top priorities. I vowed I would never again put us in the situation of being homeless, even if I had to work 24 hours a day.

By now, I recognized that I was good at developing a plan when things went awry, but I only went into planning mode after the fact. Thankfully, my best friend at the time convinced me to look much further ahead; I had to develop the branches and sequels *before* I needed them. In order to do that, I first had to identify and list the most important items and then prioritize. I started making these long lists but soon discovered that they just kept getting longer, and I never made progress. Why? If accomplishment was based simply on reducing the list, it was not happening; therefore, I had to develop some other methods to achieve my goals. Right around this time, I came across author Steven Covey and his book, *The 7 Habits of Highly Effective People.*

I studied Covey's philosophy and bought the planner to help me become more effective. His method helped me to focus on what was most important, based on intention: the 7 habits, if practiced, were simple, effective and powerful. This book became a driving factor in making a significant paradigm shift. My personal transformation affected every part of my life and allowed me to define my priorities to put the right things first. I developed priorities that represented the major areas in my life. At no given time did I list more than five, because any more than that made the task seem impossible. Once I defined my priorities, I was able to develop goals to address these areas of focus. I ensured that my plan covered my career, education, family, work, health, and spirituality. The biggest concept that emerged for me was his proactive model, highlighted by Covey's key comment, "Our behavior is a function of our decisions, not our conditions." This was such a profound and needed revelation at that time; this one statement helped me to learn how to leverage my God-given power – the freedom to choose instead of being held hostage to my past or even my current environment. This book is a staple on my bookshelf today because the concepts remain relevant over a two decades later.

Seeing Beyond the Treetops – Visioning

By the time 1995 rolled around, I had remarried, given birth to my second daughter, finished my bachelor's degree, become a commissioned officer in the National Guard, and started working for one of the largest global consulting firms. I strongly believe that learning how to prioritize and set goals contributed significantly to these achievements. While things were going well, it still seemed like I was functioning on the lower branches of the tree because I did not have a vision tied to my hopes and dreams. While I had made significant progress, I am not sure I was focused on nurturing my future growth until this point. This was when my consulting career took me to another tree in a much larger forest that I could not see because I did not even realize it existed.

I met new people, inside and outside of the company. I started joining and participating in organizations that added to my knowledge base. The firm challenged me every step of the way to stay focused on the business, become the best, and reach for the stars. No, I'm not saying everything was perfect; just that I learned to seize opportunities as they presented themselves. I developed the ability to think globally and act locally, a principle that applies to my current daytime role. When I went to my first training session with the firm at our central training location in Chicago, I was somewhat overwhelmed by the whole scene. In many respects, it was like a college campus. I had never experienced company training of this caliber, with people from all over the world. As I attended more and more sessions, I learned much from my counterparts. What I thought was unbelievably amazing is that how we all could work together to solve the problems we were confronting.

The skills I acquired easily transferred into my work

environment, civilian life, and military role. As a result of my experiences, I learned how to see beyond the current issues. Throughout this training, I not only learned how to solve problems, I developed an aptitude for critical thinking. To say that the next decade expanded my horizons would be an understatement: I not only came into my own but soared to new heights. One of my assignments was working with a partner who was a former Under Secretary for the Department of Defense and a Harvard graduate. While his resume was impressive, his strengths were in the area of strategy. I worked with him for four-to-five years, starting out on his team as the Program Manager for our work with the Army. My strengths were tactically and operationally focused in the business environment. While I understood our business, I learned to think more strategically, and how to create a vision for our teams and our client. I remember telling him at the beginning of our collaboration, "I am not the strategic thinker, you are." Finally, he came to me one day and announced that he was not in agreement; he felt that I was a strategic thinker because he had seen me exhibit those skills in many environments. Essentially, he asked me to stop saying I wasn't and to start believing in what I was doing. Thanks in part to his feedback and encouragement, I realized I was a visionary, one who was sometimes way ahead of others in identifying a solution to a problem. My challenge was communicating that vision and strategy in a manner that enabled others to get to the same place. While I have always had an innate ability to focus on the broader picture when needed, I can easily delve into the details. This was definitely a revelation and something that I still need to remain highly cognizant about.

Around this time, I developed an appreciation for the nexus of my civilian and military career. The synergy between them created unparalleled growth in all areas of my life. I began to dream big – thus, seeing beyond the tree tops, while remaining in the present moment where I continued to strengthen my foundation. One of the major goals around this time was addressing the inner me. It became a top priority, and I soon learned it was more than a one-day effort: I had to work on clearing the old leaves from the branches and remove the dead branches in order to facilitate new growth. This was significantly more work than first anticipated, but it's an ongoing task and a recurring theme. Addressing the past by examining my feelings and determining I needed just to let it go was crucial; if I didn't take the time to do it, that dreadful little monster would rear its ugly head at the most inopportune time. I could not afford for that to happen, so I listed out my feelings and decided how I would deal with them. This is definitely where forgiveness comes in.

As I discussed before, forgiveness does not always mean saying you're sorry or keeping the offending person in your life. Rather, it's about identifying those things that are weighing you down in terms of your feelings, beliefs, values, emotions, relationships, or any other significant area of life. You have to dig deep and be honest with yourself in order to define these affected areas. For me, it was a tough process. In fact, it is a continuous challenge to this day. I had come to an understanding of behaviors I don't tolerate well, along with an understanding as to how, where, and why they manifested, if at all possible. The thing about forgiveness is that it's about forgiving yourself for feeling the way you do about a person, situation, or even yourself. For me, I also realized I could make my own choices as to the folks I surrounded myself with, and when and how to engage with family or others – *if* I wanted to. Recognizing that I could choose was an important aspect in understanding my limits and setting my boundaries. I also had to be comfortable with the fact that I was doing this for me; the focus was not to please everyone else, which is counterproductive and impossible.

As a result, I am at peace with my life and appreciate the adversity of the wonderful past that has shaped me into the woman and human being I am today. I uncovered the things that gave me joy – my husband, daughters, extended family, stability, education, and ability to call the shots affecting my own life. I discovered my strengths and focused on using them in all aspects as a leader. After putting my civilian career on hold and going on two deployments, I learned more about myself than ever before. Both times away in uniform provided an opportunity for me to deal with the things that were still holding the real me back in some way. During these periods, my faith in myself was tested and I found out what was really important to me. By the second deployment, I realized what I wanted to stand for and what I wanted my legacy to be. I just had to take a step back and gain a little perspective in order to see that there was a huge forest out there. That's when I made the decision to be transparent and share my life story with the rest of the world in the event that I could inspire others. In fact, it became vital for me to be prepared to share the uncomfortable as well as the comfortable. I was not looking for a pity party; just the simple acknowledgment that life happens whether we want it to or not. Acknowledging that no matter how much we try, we may not always be in control of the events; however, we can certainly control our own actions and reactions. We do not have to surrender ourselves to the pain, disappointment, or anger, nor must we sacrifice ourselves for others. By writing my story, I wanted to demonstrate that we all have choices.

It's Your Legacy – Own It

When I think back over the years, I could not have dreamed of a life as blessed as the one I've been privileged to live. I am truly thankful for the experiences I've had, but even more thankful for those who have crossed my path. I have been touched by so many people; hopefully, I have paid it forward by touching many others with something that inspires them to be better than they are today. Even though my life took me on many twists and turns, I made deliberate choices that altered its direction on many occasions.

These intentional decisions made a significant impact in moving forward – whether I knew it or not.

Most significant was joining the military. This decision allowed many more doors to open for me than what may have been possible otherwise. Although I'd go on to make many more choices, this is the foundational one, from which everything else sprouted. It was my center of gravity out of which all else pivoted. As events unfolded, I adjusted, but the critical lesson I learned is that you can help to crystallize your plan by thinking through your decisions in advance.

You often hear people say, "Live life to the fullest." For me, it meant living the life I desired to have and refusing to allow others to set the agenda. I will have no regrets because I did everything I set out to do and had a hand in creating a life legacy I can be proud of. While it was fraught with much adversity, it was mine. We can all live life to the fullest by being intentional with our thoughts, behaviors, and actions.

I chose to focus on the things that were within my control and let go of those that were not. When a branch would break (as it often did along the way), I simply reached for the next one. Visualizing how I wanted a particular situation or event to play out helped me push forward beyond the fears and limiting beliefs that incapacitated me. Fear is insidious: it's not always apparent how it traps us into standing still and embracing the status quo instead of moving out of our comfort zone. A clear example from my own life of the paralyzing power of fear was when I took swimming lessons. Being terrified of water, I made the decision to learn how to swim as a way of overcoming the phobia. I'd even set a goal for myself to do a triathlon at some point. After about five months of lessons, I was swimming pretty well in the pool, so I decided I was ready to work with an open water swim coach. Now keep in mind, at this point, I *could* swim.

When it was time for her to assess my skills, she instructed me to walk out into the water and swim. As soon as I got out about 15-to-20 feet, the water was deep and dark, and I felt an overwhelming panic come over me. I could not catch my breath. I could not get my stroke to smooth out, and I just lost it. When I rolled onto my back, which was my safe position, she saw the fear in my face and began to talk with me as she came to the rescue and helped me back to the lake bank. As we sat by the water's edge, I was shaking. I knew my lessons were done for the day. Once safely back in my car, I cried for being so stupid and letting fear take control. I am still working on my swimming skills but have yet to conquer the open water. However, I'm still committed to making it happen because I refuse to let fear win.

In choosing to live my life on my terms, I have forgiven many people to forge a clearer path. I did not have a hidden agenda, which is detrimental to the achievement of anything good and only tends to spoil everything. I practiced restraint and avoided the trap of thinking I could do better than someone else in any particular role. I did not criticize others in their job performance because I recognized that I was not as familiar with the circumstances of the situation. This doesn't mean I had no aspirations for someday assuming these roles; simply that I didn't undermine the person in order to get there. Instead, I learned from their mistakes and fostered growth in the processes they'd originated. My current role is a perfect example: I wanted to learn as much about what my predecessors did before me as I possibly could. I wanted to know what worked well and what did not. I sought out their advice and counsel to ensure that I understood past decisions. However, I did not allow us to stay with the status quo if it meant we had to sacrifice a growth opportunity for the organization.

I did choose to do things differently because being different is what makes you stand out. I was never comfortable with just being because I knew that there was more to it than I could see.

Before I could figure out how to accentuate my strengths to transform into the best me I possibly could, I had to first develop a deeper appreciation for myself, then identify and understand my strengths. Along the way, I encouraged many others to do the same so that they could develop and grow. I simply go after what I want because not doing so means I am potentially conforming and settling for mediocrity. While this doesn't entail living on the edge, it does involve taking risks and refusing to give up. I developed the internal fortitude and ability to push past self-defeating thoughts from that little monster like, "I can't do it." Such fortitude is what I call "true grit."

I stopped living my life on autopilot many years ago when I realized that nothing, absolutely *nothing* would be handed to me. Amidst all of the criticism from others, I tried to see myself as they did, which was revealing. By obtaining their feedback, journaling, visualizing what I wanted to be, do, and have, and taking time for overall self-reflection, I discovered useful information on how to make lasting improvements for myself in order to reach my goals. I found the time to cultivate the ideas and develop my plan. At times, this effort demanded that I either limit my exposure or disassociate completely with negative or unsupportive individuals, including family members. As I have come to realize, all things and situations change; nothing is permanent. But if you have not made progress on your goals, you may need to determine what is truly standing in your way. You can make a difference if you are willing to work at it. Think about the life you want to create, then build your plan for its creation. Don't let life just pass you by without taking advantage of what it has to offer. With the understanding that the choices we make can and will impact our plan, and thus our lives, we all have the ability to choose.

My life was filled with moments of choice, some good and some bad. But most importantly, they were mine.

Made in the USA
Middletown, DE
26 May 2016